DATE DUE			
JUL 26 '84			
OCT 16 1996			
FEB 17 1997			
APR 07 1997			
DEC 15 1998			
NOV 9 2 2001			

Confucius,

His Life and Time

Confucius,

His Life and Time

By Liu Wu-Chi

Director, Department of Chinese
Studies, Hartwick College

GREENWOOD PRESS, PUBLISHERS
WESTPORT, CONNECTICUT

Library of Congress Cataloging in Publication Data

Liu, Wu-chi, 1907-
    Confucius, his life and time.

    Bibliography: p.
    1. Confucius.
[B128.C8L56 1972]   299'.5126'4 [B]   73-138159
ISBN 0-8371-5616-5

Originally published in 1955 by Philosophical Library,
New York

Reprinted with the permission of Philosophical Library, Inc

Reprinted from an original copy in the collections of the
University of Illinois Library

Reprinted in 1974 by Greenwood Press, Inc.,
51 Riverside Avenue, Westport, CT 06880

Library of Congress catalog card number 73-138159
ISBN 0-8371-5616-5

Printed in the United States of America

10 9 8 7 6 5 4 3

Great is K'ungtzu, philosopher,
The primal Seer, the primal Sage!
With Heaven and Earth he equal ranks,
Immortal Guide for every age.
Once hailed by wreathed unicorn,
Respond we now with harps and bells;
Celestial light he has revealed,
Above, below, order prevails.

—Hymn to Master K'ung.*

* This is the first stanza of the Hymn "Welcoming the Spirit," sung at sacrifices in the Confucian temple. The English version is by William E. Soothill.

"Par quelle fatalité, honteuse peut-être pour les peuples occidentaux, faut-il aller au bout de l'Orient pour trouver un sage simple, sans faste, sans imposture, qui enseignait aux hommes à vivre heureux, six cents avant notre ère vulgaire, dans un temps où tout le Septentrion ignorait l'usage des lettres, et où les Grecs commençaient à peine à se distinguer par la sagesse? Ce sage est Confucius, qui étant legislateur ne voulut jamais tromper les hommes. Quelle plus belle règle de conduite a-t-on jamais donnée depuis lui dans la terre entière?"

—Voltaire.

"Superior and alone Confucius stood,
Who taught that useful science—to be good."

—Pope.

"His whole doctrine tends to the Propagation of Virtue, and the Restitution of Human Nature to its original Perfection."

—Dr. Johnson.

Contents

Preface

IN PAST CENTURIES, K'UNG CH'IU, THE GREATEST TEACHER OF antiquity, has been grossly misrepresented. Wrapped in the mists of time and the incense of adoration, his true self has appeared but dimly to his numerous admirers. Then, as the ages glided by, even more distorted and obscure became the facts of his life and the truth of his words. In consequence, a great deal of misunderstanding arose. This is apparent in the treatment he received in the Western countries, where K'ung Ch'iu, under the Latinized name of Confucius, has often been regarded as the founder of a religion, which he decidedly is not. All this is a matter of regret, and a sad reflection on modern scholarship. Indeed, though the original materials are all there—thanks to the persistent efforts of the ancient Chinese—few people have cared to delve into them and to reconstruct therefrom the life and times of this most remarkable man. The first aim of my book is, therefore, to rediscover the *historical* K'ung Ch'iu as he lived in those dark, restless days of decaying feudalism.

I have also endeavored to present the *human* K'ung Ch'iu, a struggling scholar-official, whose lot might be that of any of us, as distinguished from the exalted, saintly figure that he has long assumed in the Chinese imagination. In other words, it is my second aim to restore K'ung Ch'iu from his mummified state into a man of flesh and blood. This is by no means an easy task, considering that he has been so long embalmed and transformed beyond recognition by the concerted efforts of the idolatrous scholars and patronizing emperors. Overwhelming indeed were the odds, and the best I could do was to visualize K'ung Ch'iu in my waking dreams, as he himself had once envisioned the renowned Duke of Chou, until gradually the dim image of the man began to emerge and then to focalize in my vision. Now I seemed to see him as he moved about in the feudal society of his time. I entered into his personality and discovered his foibles as well as his virtues. I deplored his intolerant attitude towards women and serfs; I revolted against his priggishness at court; I laughed heartily at his quixotic fight against the rising forces of a great social upheaval; and I was more than delighted and warmed by the genial and inspiring manner in which he led the younger generation and, in fact, the entire Chinese people, towards a truer way of living.

The life of K'ung Ch'iu, the *pedagogue,* especially left a deep impression upon me. I now came to understand why he was so great after all. It was not because he was a moralist or administrator, though as both he was remarkable, but because he was first of all a teacher, the greatest of his generation as well as of the myriads of generations since his time. Thus we see in him the epitome of a great culture, a man who preserved for posterity the treasured heritage of ancient China, and who established the remarkable tradition of Chinese scholarship, a tradition so far unparalleled in the intellectual history of the world. Moreover, much of his educational theory and practice is still surprisingly modern and progressive, though the contents of his teaching may have been obsolete with the lapse of time. Even so, no one can doubt the sincerity of his conception of *jen* (here translated as "human-heartedness") as an all-embracing virtue for all men, and his dream of a Great Commonwealth, the noblest and yet the most practicable Utopia which the human mind has ever conceived, and towards which all human effort should be constantly directed.

I feel sorry for K'ung Ch'iu that he has been so frequently misunderstood both at home and abroad. I feel disappointed that on this memorable occasion of the 2,500th anniversary of his birth, so little has been written about him, and that little, with a notable exception or two, is so unworthy of the Master himself. Has the attention of men been so unhappily diverted by the terrific uproar of war and atomic destruction that they have become deaf to the sweet voices of reason and truth? Or is it because men have been so accustomed to the baubles and glamor of this materialistic world that they no longer care about the genuine worth of an old-fashioned scholar, whose chief attractions are his wisdom and erudition? In any case, as a teacher myself, who believes in the dignity of learning and experiences the happiness of imparting knowledge, I have attempted here, in spite of my shortcomings, to pay my tribute, which is due, or rather overdue, to Master K'ung Ch'iu, the great founder of a noble and honorable profession.

LIU WU-CHI

First of all, I wish to express my obligations to the various translators of the Confucian Classics, from which I quote profusely. My original plan was to give independent renderings of my own, but my efforts compared so unfavorably with those of the previous scholars that I was finally persuaded to use their translations whenever they were better than mine. I have been careful, however, in collating all the quotations with the original texts and making whatever revisions I deemed necessary in order to keep the translated passages closer to the original and make them read more smoothly. Hence I am responsible for any mistakes herein. As it would take too much space and time to enumerate all the sources of my debt, I am making a general acknowledgement instead.

Secondly, I am indebted to many friends in China, who sent me in the past years the necessary material for the compilation of this book. I am sorry to say that the high cost of printing Chinese characters makes it impossible to add here a bibliography of the Chinese works I have used.

I also want to take this chance to thank all my friends who have shown a kind interest in this work. In particular, my gratitude goes to the Bollingen Foundation in New York for a grant-in-aid; to Mrs. Willard Church, a devoted friend of China and the Chinese, for her generous help and encouragement; to Virginia G. Collins, herself an author and a lover of Chinese culture, for having painstakingly gone over the entire manuscript.

Last but not least, my thanks are due to my wife, about whom traditional Chinese modesty forbids me from making any further compliment.

Confucius,

His Life and Time

CHAPTER ONE

The Year 551 B.C.

1. *An Unsceptered King Is Born*

THERE WAS NOTHING AUSPICIOUS OR SPECTACULAR ABOUT THE year 551[1] before the Christian era, when a male child was born to the family of K'ung in the small dukedom of Lu about two hundred miles eastward to the Yellow Sea. A legion of wondrous tales, to be sure, did spring up around this new-born baby after it had become the greatest sage of China, an unsceptered king in the realm of letters. But for this event, that particular year, like any other of the eight hundred years and more during the long reign of the House of Chou, might have gone by entirely unnoticed.

It was, however, the beginning of an important epoch in

1. There are two dates of K'ung Ch'iu's birth: one, according to Kung-yang and Ku-liang (two 5th century B.C. commentators of the *Spring and Autumn* annals by K'ung Ch'iu), on the 21st year of Duke Hsiang of Lu (B.C. 552); and another, according to Ssu-ma Ch'ien (a famous 1st century B.C. historian), on the 22nd year of Duke Hsiang (B.C. 551). Much controversy has been raised on this question by Chinese scholars of the last twenty centuries. The date now generally, but not unanimously, accepted, is that given by Ssu-ma Ch'ien.

The question of the dates is further complicated by James Legge, the English Sinologist, who made the mistake of one year in all his chronological statements in his translation of *Chinese Classics* by not counting the year of Christ's birth as 1 B.C. (See F. Hirth, *Ancient History of China*, p. 174.) Thus Legge, while following Kung-yang and Ku-liang in dating K'ung Ch'iu's birth on the 21st year of Duke Hsiang, wrongly assigned it to the year 551 B.C. The mistake was followed by many other Sinologists and persisted even as late as 1948 in Maurice Collis' *The First Holy One*. Collis followed Ssu-ma Ch'ien but gave 550 B.C. as the 22nd year of Duke Hsiang, instead of the correct 551 B.C.

the intellectual history of China. As a matter of fact, the
Chinese people, whose rude forefathers first picked up the
rudiments of civilization some two and a half millenniums
before, grew up to manhood with the K'ung child. The latter,
in turn, exerted such a moulding influence upon Chinese life
that it continued in the same pattern for yet another two millenniums and a half until the present day. Thus the year 551
B.C. was, in fact, a significant date, and the birth of the K'ung
child a tremendous event, in the development of the Chinese
people and their culture. But before we turn to the life and
times of this peerless personality, let us pause first for a picture of the historical background, against which the "baby"
was born and brought up.

2. *The Feudal Pyramid*

The K'ung child entered the scene during a short interlude
between the acts of a great, colorful, and throbbing drama,
that endless drama of man's struggle for existence and achievement, heightened now and then by the alarums of war and
the decline and fall of hoary empires. The setting of our particular drama was placed in the central plains of the Middle
Kingdom, east and south of the great southern bend of the
Yellow River, the cradle of Chinese civilization. It occurred
in an age of feudalism, somewhat similar in outline to that
of medieval Europe some fifteen hundred years later, but
with the striking difference that here in China, instead of
knights-errant on prancing steeds, there were itinerant scholars with cartloads of bamboo tablets, the books of the time,[2] on
their way to some feudal court in quest of sage-rulers. The
principal actors, who entered and left the stage in each act,

2. The ancient Chinese books consisted of a bundle of bamboo tablets, on
which were inscribed the written characters. These slips were bound together
by a leather thong. Books were still very rare in K'ung Ch'iu's time. It was only
after his death in the time of the Warring States (5th to 3rd century B.C.) that
scholars possessed wagonfuls of bamboo books, their personal library, which
they carried along as they travelled from one state to another.

were the feudal lords who traced their ancestry to some remote hero or king, and, in many cases, to some relation or
lineal descendant of the reigning house of Chou.

It all came about in this way: Some five and a half centuries
before the birth of the great child, the Chou dynasty had been
founded by its renowned kings, Wen, the Civilized, and his
son Wu, the Martial, with the help of Wu's younger brother,
the sagacious Duke of Chou. The Martial King, having sub-
jugated the Shang people, who had formerly ruled the Chinese domain, established himself as the Heavenly King[3] of
the new regime. After his death, the Duke of Chou consoli-
dated the kingdom by leading impressive expeditions eastward and southward to extend far and wide the royal sway.
The myriad tribes of the hills and plains were awed into sub-
mission, and as a result, the loosely knitted communities of
the then civilized China were welded together under the central authority of the Chou sovereign. The clan heads and
tribal chieftains friendly to Chou were allowed to retain the
lands they formerly held on the outskirts of the Chinese
demesne, but most of the conquered territories of Shang on
the great plains were apportioned anew to the members of
the royal family, ministers and generals of merit, and the offspring of ancient rulers, so that they might continue uninter-
rupted the sacrifices to their great ancestors.

These new fiefs[4] were distributed on a scale proportional
to the ranks of the recipients in the feudal hierarchy,—the

3. The king of Chou was commonly known as the Son of Heaven, a title later
adopted by Chinese emperors. But in K'ung Ch'iu's *Spring and Autumn*, the
Chou sovereign was invariably referred to as the "Heavenly King." In Legge's
translation, the term becomes "King, (by the grace of) Heaven," thus losing
much of the original significance.

4. There is no reliable account of the exact number of vassals enfeoffed by
the Chou kings. According to scholarly calculations, there were as many as 1773
states, large and small, in the heyday of Chou feudalism. (See Y. P. Mei, *Motse,
Rival of Confucius*, London, 1934, p. 14.) This mathematical figure is of course
unfounded, but there is no doubt that the number of fiefs was a very large

baronies, viscountcies, earldoms, marquisdoms, and duchies thus created ranging in size from fifty to a hundred square li.[5] Clustering together like luxuriant underbrush, they formed a "screen and fence" for the large royal domain that stretched for a thousand square li in the hub of the Chinese universe with its two capitals, Hao (near Sian) and Lo (Loyang), strategically situated to the west and east of the Yellow River valley. "All below Heaven, is it not the king's land?" sang an anonymous poet of that period.

The feudal prince, who received his fief from the Son of Heaven, presided over his estate like a quasi-independent ruler with a miniature court imitative of the royal pattern, an ancestral temple where elaborate sacrifices were performed to obtain blessings from the manes of his noble forefathers, and an army of varying strength measured by the number of armored chariots that could be mustered in time of war. In his own principality, the lord had absolute sway over his subjects and subordinates; but he, like his fellow aristocrats, owed allegiance to the Chou suzerain, to whom he paid homage and offered tribute, and at whose summons he raised an army to take part in a royal campaign. The king, as the supreme overlord, from whom all feudal authority emanated, had the

one, if we are to include all the small communities welded together by the chieftains and tribal heads in the outskirts of the Chou kingdom.

From a statement in the *Tso's Commentary* (another commentary on the *Spring and Autumn* traditionally attributed to Tso Ch'iu-ming, circa 5th century B.C.) we know that "when King Wu subdued Shang, and obtained grand possession of all the lands, 15 of his brothers and 40 other princes of the surname of Chi (the royal clan) received states" (Legge, *Chinese Classics*, V, 192.) There were many other members of the Chi clan endowed with fiefs in the later reigns. We are on more certain grounds when we come to the beginning of the Eastern Chou dynasty (circa 700 B.C.). At that time, there were still approximately 200 states, the names of which can be found in the historical records of the period. (See Ch'ien Mu, *Outlines of Chinese National History*, Shanghai, 1948, I, 44. Y. P. Mei gives the number of states as 160 in *Motse*, p. 16.)

5. In the early days of Chou enfeoffment, a feudatory was very small. Even a dukedom of a hundred square li is only a little over 11 square miles in territory, a li being about one third of a mile.

right to invest a new feudatory with a fief as well as to unseat any of his vassals who misbehaved or misgoverned. In the good old days when the Son of Heaven was at the height of his power, such royal prerogatives were actually exercised. History gives us several instances of aristocratic miscreants who were deprived of their rank and fief; records also show that some were very severely punished for their insubordination.

Under the enfeoffed rulers lived the lesser nobles, who were hereditary ministers at the feudal court, governors of outlying townships, and mailed warriors in times of war. As subvassals, they held in fief strips of land parcelled out by their lord, and stood in the same relation to him as he to the king. Further down, at the broad, massive base of the feudal pyramid, formed by the five-tiered nobility with the Heavenly King at its apex, was a class of aristocracy, the lowest in the hierarchy, called *shih*.[6] Many of these lived at court as minor officials, filling the less important posts in the feudal bureaucracy. Others became village heads, and acted, in that capacity, as land-supervisors and tax-collectors for the prince and his ministers. They thus served as a useful link between the great aristocracy at the top of the social strata and the mass of common people at the very bottom—that vast agricultural population that tilled the land and fed the nation.

The *shih* were, as a whole, educated and intelligent. Like their superiors, they drew their revenue from the land or received for their services emoluments from their lord. They lived a life of comparative ease, but they were not rich enough to be spoiled by the luxury and sensual indulgence that contributed to the gradual decadence of the great aristocratic

6. Waley's translation of *shih* as "knight" in his version of the *Analects* is misleading. There are several meanings to the word "knight," and Waley has in mind probably its meaning as a non-hereditary rank next below a baronet. But it would be fantastic to imagine K'ung Ch'iu, who was also a *shih*, as a medieval knight, who devoted himself chivalrously to the cause of distressed ladies.

families. Though noble by birth, they were in fact the bour-
geoisie of feudal society, from which came scholars and philosophers, statesmen and diplomats. Also from this class came
the child K'ung. But with the dissolution of the feudal system
in later days, the word *shih* lost its original meaning as the
title of a non-hereditary official, the lowest grade of nobility,
and became identified in its new usage with the scholar-official
class, the men of letters, who were destined to play a vital
role in the future administration of the Chinese government.

3. *Those Hereditary Intellectuals*

Attached to the feudal court and likewise educated, were a
group of hereditary diviners, historiographers, and music masters, who too might have been tutors of ceremonies to the
youthful lordlings. With the ancient rulers, divination was an
extremely important practice, from which they sought guid-
ance in state affairs, and by means of which they regulated
their life and activities. To divine is to resolve doubt. Would
a particular day be auspicious for hunting or expedition?
Would it rain to relieve a long drought and the threat of
dearth and famine? And, even more important, would
Heaven, or the gods of Land and Grain,[7] or the powerful ancestral spirits of the royal family be gracious enough to grant
deliverance from the menacing calamities of the day such as
the eclipse of the sun, the falling of meteors, and the incursion
of barbaric tribes? Indeed, could their divine blessings be in-
voked and relied upon on the eve of a great battle, when the
baronial army was about to sally forth to meet an enemy attack?

7. The gods of Land (or Soil) and Grain, probably of agricultural origin,
were the chief deities in the Chou time. To worship them, there was erected
in each feudal capital an altar on a raised mound, which soon became the
symbolic religious center of the community. Later, the term became synonymous with the state itself,—a state fell when its altar of Land and Grain was
destroyed.

The proper course of action for such weighty affairs was usually sought from indications on the tortoise shell or the way in which the milfoil stalks grouped themselves.[8] Tortoise divination was practised as early as the Shang dynasty. Its belly surface having been carefully incised with a red-hot stylus, the tortoise shell was held before a scorching fire until cracks formed, from which oracular utterances were read and made public. Later, in the Chou times, a new process of augury was devised with the use of a fixed number of milfoil sticks arranged in a definite order, the judgment for every possible combination and permutation of the sticks having been previously made and recorded in a work of divination known as the *Book of Changes*. Charged with such tremendous duties, the diviners, who were hereditary experts in their profession, formed an indispensable part of the court appanage. From their center of activity in the ancestral temple, of which they were guardians, they exerted considerable influence over the affairs of their lord and his state. Through the mysterious signs on the divining shell and by means of the stalks, they spoke as the deputies of spirits and deities, while their words of warning were listened to and heeded.

In almost every feudal court there were also historiographers who served as personal secretaries to the reigning prince. These kept his speeches and actions on record, and prepared for him diplomatic notes to be sent to the neighboring lords on interstate affairs. As keepers of the court archives, they had recourse to the fountainhead of historical knowledge, other-

8. A very interesting story about the relative merits of the two methods of Chou divination is told in the *Tso's Commentary* under the 4th year of Duke Hsi of Lu (B.C. 656). When Duke Hsien of Tsin was about to make his favorite concubine, Lady Li of the barbaric Jung tribe, his wife, he referred the matter to divination. "The tortoise-shell indicated that it would be unlucky, but the milfoil pronounced it lucky. The duke said, 'I will follow the milfoil.' The diviner by the tortoise-shell said, 'The milfoil is reckoned inferior in its indications to the tortoise-shell. You had better follow the latter.'" But the duke did not listen to his advice, and in consequence, the state was thrown into great turmoil after his death. (Legge, *Chinese Classics*, V, 141.)

wise inaccessible; and equipped with this unusual information, they became, to a future generation, the transmitters of learning and culture. Their primary task, however, was that of historical compilation; hence they may be called the earliest official writers in China.

As historians, they chronicled, in the form of annals, all the important events that took place in and around the lord's domain,—the birth, ascension, and death of a feudal lord; a marriage in the aristocratic family, when, for instance, the duke's daughter went to the harem of a neighboring earl; the presentation by the Heavenly King of carriages and horses for a ducal funeral; formal visits from the envoy of a friendly state with conciliatory offerings of silk and jade; the meeting of the princes, and the covenant which they swore to by daubing their mouth with the sheep's blood; the acceptance of an heirloom bronze tripod as bribery from a usurping prince, and the remonstrance of a faithful minister against its being placed in the Grand Temple. Also recorded were such natural disturbances as floods and torrential rains, terrific thunder and lightning storms, snowstorms, falling stars and eclipses, and devastating locust plagues. And, above all, in these historical pages was presented *la tragedic humaine* of wars and murders, now becoming more and more frequent towards the second half of the 6th century B.C.

The feudal court in the Chou period was probably the most musical of all the ancient courts. Almost all grand ceremonials were accompanied by melodious performances. Every occasion had its special kind of music. There was music for the sacrifices at the ancestral temple, the archery contest, the capping ceremony for boys, and the coiffure ceremony for girls. It too was played in entertainments and feasts, in which military dancers performed their nimble movements with shields and hatchets, and civil dancers trod their rhythmical measures with gorgeously colored pheasant feathers and pennants of ox-tails.

Even at their daily meals, the princes had musicians, some of whom were blind, playing for them. In the ducal court of Lu, home of the K'ung child, which enjoyed the royal prerogative on account of its great founder, the Duke of Chou,[9] a different bandmaster attended on the prince during each of his four meals, the rulers of the other states having only three.

The Chou music was quite advanced in its development with eight different classes of instruments: the bells that ring clear and resonant; the musical stone (*ch'ing,* a stone slab suspended in a stand) with its sharp and clear-cut sound; the string instruments (*ch'in* and *sê,* which are zithers, having fifty or less strings over a perforated, horizontal sounding board) in a plaintive, soul-cleansing tone; the bamboo instrument (flute) with its floating quality; the noise-making drums and timbrels; the gourd-shaped *sheng* (a mouth organ with bamboo reedpipes); the clay pipes; and the square wooden-boxes.

Each of these instruments was played by an expert musician under the direction of the "grand-master." Like the diviner and the historiographer, he was an hereditary intellectual in the aristocratic household. Since music was closely akin to rites, it is quite possible that the "grand-master" was also the ritual expert at court, who in that capacity might even have tutored the young princes in ceremonials as well as in music. It is interesting to note here the ancient usage of prefixing the word *shih* (master or teacher) to the name of the music-master. Might it not be that he too was the predecessor of the K'ung child, who later became the foremost teacher of ceremonies in the millennium-old educational history of China?

4. *The Six Arts*

Unlike the unlettered barons of medieval Europe, the Chou rulers were taught in their early life the rudiments of the

9. Actually, the first duke of Lu was Po Ch'in (B.C. 1115?–1063?), son of the Duke of Chou.

"six arts": charioteering and archery, history and numbers, music and rituals. Poetry, it seems, was also studied, as on many a diplomatic occasion, both hosts and visitors had on the tip of their tongues verses illustrative of the discourses and arguments in which they were politely engaged. All these, apparently, were regarded as part and parcel of a prince's education, and, for this purpose, the services of accomplished tutors were enlisted.

In war and hunting, the favorite pastimes of an aristocrat, skill in chariot-driving and archery was indispensable. When it was the season for the grand chase, the noble lord, heading a long bannered train, rode in his trim, stoutly made hunting carriage, to which was harnessed four superb and richly caparisoned horses. With a ring on the right thumb to protect it from the bow string, and a glove on the left hand and wrist to guard these against the arrows in shooting, the aristocratic bowman dispatched his deadly shots, each shaft hurtling like an axe at the deer, fox, wild-cat, raccoon, badger, and other game kept on his hunting grounds.

In wartime, the feudal prince took personal command of the field. Mounted on his two-wheeled carriage[10] drawn by four armored steeds, with bells jingling and ornaments glittering, the martial lord stood in the center of his box-like coach with an archer on the left and a lancer on the right, while he held in his hand the six reins that guided the movement of the horses, and with it the movement of the entire army. The other chariots, their horses blanketed with the skins of wild beasts, were manned by aristocratic warriors who wore varnish-glazed

10. The war chariots were short and narrow, formed by a box open at the back and mounted on two wheels. In front was a curved pole, to which two shaft-horses were fastened: on each side two outside horses were kept at a distance by side-straps. The four chariot horses were provided with bits to which two little bells were fixed. The reins were attached to these bits: the inner reins of the two outside horses were fastened behind the two rings placed right and left of the board which formed the front of the chariot; the other reins were held by the driver. (Marcel Granet, *Chinese Civilization*, p. 263.)

rhinoceros cuirasses and who were protected in the front by shields of light wood. These men did the actual fighting with axe and spear, lance and halberd, and above all, with bow and arrow, while foot soldiers, conscripted mainly from among the large bulk of farm laborers, followed in their wake to carry provisions, camp equipment, and the various impedimenta needed in a military campaign.

Archery, it must be noted, was as much an art of peace as an art of war. There were official contests presided over by the king or the lord, and private contests for fun and recreation, accompanied by feasting, drinking, and music. In a ritualistic tournament, archery was also the great test of nobility. Every shot from the bow had to be synchronized with music, and every movement of the contestant regulated by a set of elaborate rules. The match was a sort of team competition, with two bands of archers vying with each other, three against three. The paired competitors bowed and yielded precedence as they contended. From their strong and brightly varnished bows, they each sent four well-poised shafts at the target. Their bearing was then judged as each took his final place. At last, after the result of the contest had been announced by the master of ceremonies, the noble losers graciously emptied the wine cup passed around in acknowledgment of their defeat.

· For his intellectual enlightenment, the young lord was given instruction in numbers, probably connected with divination, and history, in the form of documents and annals. Music was also a required study, as its performance accompanied all ceremonies, whether they were in the nature of a religious sacrifice, a court assembly, or a family entertainment. But most important of all was the code of rituals and etiquette, known as *li*, that governed the moral, social, and religious activities of the entire world of aristocracy. Just as land ownership was the economic foundation of the feudal system, so was the observance of *li* its ethical prop. It permeated and pervaded every province of a noble's life, so much so that it became synonymous with nobility itself.

Etymologically, *li* is religious in nature, the word being a combination of two elements that denote worship with a sacrificial vessel. In the course of its evolution in the 6th century B.C., when the K'ung child grew up to be the greatest master of *li*, it came to include all forms of rituals and everything in connection with the proper conduct of the aristocrat. "He is a noble," it is said, "who bears himself nobly." And to bear oneself nobly, one has to be well versed in the code of nobility, which is *li*. To guide the lord's son in his personal conduct and manners, and to instill into his young mind such a thorough dose of *li*, so that he would not overstep the bounds of decency and propriety in his daily intercourse, was therefore the main task of a tutor in the aristocratic household. If this educational program had been strictly adhered to, which was by no means the case, the princeling thus trained would indeed have become a youthful paragon of virtue! So much was expected of him, in fact, that another word, *chün-tzu*, meaning originally the "lord's son," came to have its present connotation of a "perfect gentleman."

5. *An Idyllic Scene*

On the other side of the social scale, diametrically opposed to *chün-tzu*, was *hsiao-jen*, the little fellow, or the common man. In ancient as in modern China, the overwhelming bulk of the population was comprised of farmers born to the soil, on which they worked day long and month long, year in and year out. The peasants started their labor in winter when they chose their seeds and put their farming implements in order. With the coming of spring, they went in thousands of pairs to the south-lying acres, along the dykes and in the low, wet lands, to clear away the grass and the brush, and to plow, the sharpened blades of their plowshares rising in long, unbroken lines. Then came planting time, with wheat, rice, millet, corn, pulse, hemp, and beans taking their proper places according to the locality of the fields, the season of sowing, and the immediate needs of the household. It was only a short interval before multitudes of weeders set to work, pulling out the infesting darnels and wolf's-tail, and destroying the insect pests on stem and leaf. As the hinds toiled on the southern slopes, exposed to the noonday sun's fierce heat, notwithstanding the light splint hats they tied on their brows, what a welcome sight greeted their eyes as their wives and children came bringing food and drink! Now merry voices filled the open fields as the families ate together. What a truly happy scene!

After plenty of fine weather and seasonable rainfall, the well-nourished stalks grew long. Soon the luxuriant blades eared, the young grain matured and hardened, and acres burst into flame in the mellowing autumn sun. Then came the reapers in troops to harvest the grain. Some they stored in granaries; from the rest they distilled sweet spirits to offer as libations to the shades of their ancestors. They piled high the sheaves, until hundreds, thousands, and myriads of stacks rose in a serried row as tall and strong as the city walls. They also picked the gourds, plucked the rushes, and shook down the dates, while the crickets chirped beneath their eaves. Wild plums and cherries ripened on the trees, melons on the vine, as beans and mallows hissed in the cooking pots. The climax of the harvest came when in the midst of such abundance, the husbandmen killed a tawny, crooked-horned bull as an offering to the gods; "for our fathers of yore would have thanked them thus. Shall such grateful rites be forgot by us?"

From the above idyllic scene drawn by the anonymous folk poets of the period, we see that the peasants did lead in the plentiful years a self-sufficient, and, in spite of their hard toil, a reasonably well-contented life. But even then, a good share of their crops went towards the enrichment and extravagance of the feudal lords, who enjoyed the produce of their fields as well as their services in times of war and peace. According to a prevailing view of the time, it was the duty of those who toiled with their bodies to feed those who worked only with their minds.[11] So, true to this conception, the overlords who governed the peasants ate the fruits of their labor. Together with the great retinue of artisans and traders, grooms and bondsmen, attached to the lord's household, the serfs formed a major part of the aristocratic paraphernalia. During the farming seasons, they cultivated the fields to produce food for the noble prince; in slack hours, they served him as attendants and helpers. They went, for instance, fox-hunting and wildcat-chasing to get fur for the lord's winter robe, while their women-folk stayed home to weave silk and spin hemp for his summer clothes. Sometimes they also participated in the sacrifices at the ruler's ancestral temple, thereby getting a festival meal from the remains of the lordly table. Holding aloft their drinking-cups of buffalo-horn, they pressed to their master's hall, shouting their toasts: "Hurra for our lord; may he live forever and ever!"

In the earliest days of the Chou era, when the vassalage was small, a sort of family relationship and communal life did exist between the lord and his farm-hands, who were satisfied with their humble lot and heartily enjoyed the patronage of their superiors. But such personal contact became less frequent as the feudatory grew in lands, power, and wealth. Finally, when the government machinery became complicated, a whole set of officials was employed to take charge of administrative duties. Thus a bureaucracy sprang up between the prince and his rural subjects. It was then that the vast gulf deepened be-

11. Cf. the words of Meng K'o (Mencius): "Some toil with their minds, others toil with their bodies. Those that toil with their minds govern others; those that toil with their bodies are governed by others. Those who are governed feed their fellows; those who govern are fed by their fellows." (Lionel Giles, *The Book of Mencius*, London, 1942, p. 60.)

tween the two classes of mind-laborers and body-laborers.
Whereas it is a moot question how much the aristocrats actually worked with their brains, a matter of certainty it is that
the peasants continued to till the fields with their sweat and
blood for generations and generations without any prospect of
improving their servile condition. In proportion as the unsati-
ated desires of the lords became augmented, so did the peasants' lot become more and more wretched. On very rare occasions their poignant outcries were raised as in this typical
lament of the times:

> You do not sow or reap—
> How do you get the produce of those three hundred farms?
> You do not follow the chase—
> How is it that we see badgers hanging up in your courtyards?
> Ah! the true aristocrat
> Would not eat the bread of idleness!

Long oppressed and downtrodden, the *hsiao-jen* remained,
notwithstanding these protests, a species of dumb, inarticulate
animal, whose complaints were scarcely heard, and if heard,
scarcely heeded.

6. *The Landless Class*

It is no paradox to say that the peasantry which was rooted
to the land was a landless class, since the fields they cultivated
were owned by their lord, and given them only in tenancy.
According to the traditional "well-field" system, which sounds
too good to be true, lands in a fief were divided into nine
squares of a hundred *mu*[12] each; the eight outer squares given
to eight peasant families for cultivation, each family holding a
hundred *mu* of arable land. On it they had their homestead,
consisting of a thatched hut; a well and a kitchen; a pen for
domestic animals such as dogs, fowls, pigs, sheep and oxen; a
mulberry lot; and a vegetable garden, in which they grew leeks

12. A *mu* is about one sixth of an acre.

and scallions. This was their private field, on which they worked and from the produce of which they fed their family of many mouths. In addition, the eight families tilled together the central square which section was the public field, its yearly yield going to the granary of the feudal lord, the hereditary master of the entire farm.

Whether the land was ever divided into such "well"-shaped lots is a matter of historical curiosity and scholarly controversy,[13] but it is quite plausible that a system of private and public fields did exist sometimes under the Chou feudalism. Its actual operation, as we can easily see, differed but very little from the later practice of taxing the farmer a tithe of his crops.[14] All in all, the land, on which the peasant toiled all his life to eke out a meager existence, was the chief source of revenue for the feudal prince, and it was to increase this revenue that wars of annexation were fought in our period of Chou history.

13. The "well-field" system of agriculture was mentioned in the works of Meng K'o, Ku-liang, as well as in the *Chou Rituals,* a post-K'ung classic. But European Sinologists and some modern Chinese scholars doubt on rather flimsy grounds, I think, the existence of such a system. In this connection, the following verse from the *Book of Poetry* is worth quoting:

> The clouds o'erspread the sky in masses dense,
> And gentle rain down to the earth dispense.
> First may the public fields the blessing get,
> And then with it our private fields we wet.

14. Tax was first levied in Lu from the produce of the acres in the 15th year of duke Hsuan (B.C. 594). The tax officer walked over the fields and took a tithe of their yields. (See Legge, *Chinese Classics,* V, "Prolegomena," pp. 68–9; p. 329.)

CHAPTER TWO

On the Chou Horizon

1. *The Smile That Costs a Kingdom*

TRUE TO THE OLD CHINESE SAYING THAT GREAT PROSPERITY
leads inevitably to decay, the Chou dynasty, which was built
on the ruins of Shang and had its heyday in the last years of the
second millennium before Christ, began to lose its power and
prestige as the centuries rolled on towards the time the K'ung
child was born.

The first evidence of the unpopularity of the royal house was
shown in the death of King Chao (B.C. 1052–1002), who, as
tradition has it, was drowned in a southern expedition, when
his glue-fastened boat, furnished him by his discontented subjects, fell apart midway across the mighty Han stream. His son
Mu (B.C. 1001–947) is said to have travelled westward to meet
the legendary Western Queen Mother (ingeniously identified
by a Sinologist as the Queen of Sheba) at her palace of jade on
the White Jasper Mountain. Actually, he was engaged in a
punitive campaign against the Western barbarians, from
which he brought back nothing more than the trophy of "four
wolves and four white stags." After these unsuccessful attempts
at territorial expansion, the royal authority declined. With Li,
the Oppressive (B.C. 878–842), matters grew even worse. Re-
senting criticism, he negotiated several executions in an attempt to seal the people's mouths, which was an undertaking

"more dangerous than damming the waters of a flood." Revolution and banishment were the natural results.

Then came Yu, the Gloomy (B.C. 781–771). Infatuated with a beautiful but sullen woman, Lady Ssu of Pao, he deposed in her favor his lawful queen, daughter of the Marquis of Shen. The gloomy pair must have had a boring time together, if we are to believe in historical gossip, for the lady Pao never laughed, and was only slightly amused at hearing the sound of tearing silk. In a desperate effort to win a charming smile, the king ordered the lighting of the beacon fires on the hill-top, which was the signal used to announce the approach of an enemy on the royal domain. The fire must have spread like Agamemnon's torch, for all the feudal lords came to their liege's rescue, fully armed in their gaudy chariots. Needless to say, the bewilderment and disappointment, the commotion and confusion among the bustling lords, as they converged helter-skelter below the royal palace, was certainly a great sight to see. So irresistibly funny was it to the morose lady, in fact, that she burst into laughter.

Indeed, this was the most expensive laughter that a king ever paid for. As the story goes, when later (B.C. 771) the capital was actually invaded by the barbaric Jung Dogs, who came in alliance with the Marquis of Shen to avenge his daughter's disgrace, the beacons were kindled again, but kindled in vain to bring the disgruntled feudatories to the king's aid. Yu, the Gloomy, fighting a lonely battle, was killed at the foot of the Black Horse Hill near the western capital, while his dismal queen was carried away by the Dog barbarians, who also made a goodly spoil of the imperial treasury. The Chou poet who sang in impassioned lyrics of the curse on Pao Ssu and the folly of womenfolk in general failed to see the ominous writing on the wall that doomed the existence of the Western Chou:

> The wise man's wisdom is our strength,
> Woman's wisdom is our bane.

The men build up the city walls
For women to tear down again.

No man from any woman's wit
    Hath yet learned aught of any worth,
For wise is she, but unto ill,
    To bring disorder on the earth.

What doth she in affairs of State?
    Her place is in the inner room.
Her wisdom doth least hurt in this:
    To mind the silkworm and the loom.

2. *Contributions Towards the King's Funeral*

The year 770 B.C., a pivotal year in Chinese history, saw the re-establishment of the Chou sovereignty in the east. King P'ing, the Peaceful (B.C. 770–720), who succeeded his father Yu, moved his court from Hao, the western Chou capital since the Martial King, to Lo, south of the great bend of the Yellow River. At the time of Duke Chou, about three and a half centuries before, Lo was built as a second capital to buttress the royal authority in the eastern half of the kingdom. But now, the removal of the imperial seat from Hao to Lo to avoid further inroads of the Dog barbarians, was a show of weakness on the part of the reigning house. Furthermore, it was with the help of his vassals that King P'ing was placed on the throne. The succession, however, was not a happy one supported by all the feudatories, and it was secured only after a great deal of bloodshed. Since then, the Chou authority no longer commanded awe and respect.

Even worse things happened to the tottering House of Chou. The good old illusion of the Heavenly King's being the supreme overlord of the kingdom was now once and for all shattered. With its western portion, the original seat of Chou power, lost to the barbaric tribes and later seized by the state of Ch'in, the royal domain was sadly reduced to the size of an average state. Naturally, the imperial sway suffered. Though the Chou House continued to reign in its new capital at Lo for yet another five hundred years, its rule, more nominal than actual, did not extend much beyond the royal territory. With a large part of his revenue gone, as tribute ceased to come in from the feudal lords, the Chou ruler found himself impoverished as well as impotent. Indeed, in time the imperial prestige sank so low that funds had to be raised from the rich vassals to defray the cost of burying deceased Chou sovereigns. As early as 720 B.C., to mention only one instance, on the death of P'ing, the Peaceful, an envoy was sent to Lu from the royal court to ask for a delayed contribution of money towards the king's funeral.

3. *The Tribulus on the Wall*

It is true that the decree of Heaven had not changed for the dynasty of Chou. But the feudal pyramid with the Son of Heaven at its top was being undermined from all directions. This great aristocratic structure, which had held out, for a miraculously long period of time, against "the wreckful siege of battering days," was now fast crumbling, its tiered hierarchy thrown into confusion, its political and social foundation tottering, and its moral prop, the noble code of *li,* in the process of being worm-eaten to the core. Though the old traditions still clung tenaciously to an unexpired lease of life, the general outlook on the feudal horizon was dark and disheartening.

In ancient-times, a fief consisted of a walled town with a market place, an altar to the god of the soil, an ancestral temple, a manor house; and outside, a belt of farmlands protected by other walls. Beyond the fields lay the sparsely peopled heath, wooded mountains, and marshes covered with rushes and underbrush, where the wild beasts roamed at large. There, also, the barbaric tribes made their home. Thus separated from one another by these waste lands, the feudal nobles lived in peace and enjoyed the simple luxuries their subjects furnished them. But in the course of centuries, through drainage, deforestation, and reclamation, the cultivated areas grew; productivity increased with the introduction of the iron ploughshare and other farming implements; and the nomadic tribes merged into a vast agrarian population. As a result, the feudal states expanded and touched upon each other, until there developed with the passing of time a keen rivalry, a life and death struggle for supremacy.

Then came a corresponding change in the spirit of war. The old laws of feudal encounter, based upon time-sanctioned ideals, were no longer recognized. Instead of fighting for princely honors with much pomp and ceremony, the feudal lord now waged wars for territorial expansion. Moral triumph, to be sure, was still the aim of many a campaign. Even as late as the sixth century B.C., King Chuang of Ch'u showed much of the old chivalric spirit when he spared Cheng at the sight of its penitent and humiliated earl, stripped to the waist and leading a lamb; later, he also granted an honorable peace to Sung when informed of the sad plight of its beleaguered inhabitants, who were exchanging children for food and splitting up the bones of the dead for fuel. But oftener, these humanitarian considerations failed to make an appeal, and the practical feudal prince was more interested in material aggrandizement than mere glory and prestige. In place of the captives and hostages, the jade and bronze of former victories, he now brought back the spoils of land and population.

Feudal morality, too, became a mockery of its former self. Ceremonies and etiquette, as a matter of fact, were still practised in the courts, but the spirit underlying them was gone. Gone also was the ideals of *chün-tzu,* the acme of moral perfection. In their place, the feudal rulers, with more power and revenue than the Chou king ever had, became addicted to inordinate desires and carnal pleasures. Land produced wealth, wealth led to luxury, and luxury, in turn, bred the vermin of corruption and contention, filth and lewdness, that ran riot in the aristocrat's palace and his harem. A poem of Wey,[1] describing an immoral scene in the inner apartments of the reigning marquis, epitomizes the general situation prevalent in all the other feudal courts:

> The tribulus grows on the wall,
>   Upon the stain.
> The things done in that inner room
>   Men cannot name.
>
> The tribulus grows on the wall;
>   The stain is old.
> The evil of that inner room
>   May not be told.

This was no exaggeration. Much worse deeds of moral depravity were perpetuated everywhere, drunken orgies, court intrigues, and ruthless killing being common occurrences in the chronicles of the age. The harem system, which provided the ruler with as many concubines as his fancy desired, was also the chief source of trouble. Although it was an established practice for the feudal lord to designate his eldest son the heir apparent, as was the order of succession in the Chou royal house, many a senile sensualist would, even in face of strong opposition, promote the son of a favorite concubine to the feudal seat by deposing the legitimate heir, thus creating a world of strife and bloodshed. As a result of these family dis-

1. In the romanization of the Chou states, I have followed, for the sake of clarity, C. P. Fitzgerald in his *China, A Short Cultural History*, by using Wey for a small principality in the Spring and Autumn period (B.C. 722–481), to distinguish it from Wei, one of the powerful states in the Warring States period (B.C. 403–21). I have also used Tsin to distinguish it from Ch'in, two of the great states in K'ung Ch'iu's time.

sensions, sometimes atrocious deeds, including fratricide and patricide, were committed in the princely house, leading to untold confusion.

4. *Tzu-K'ung Dips His Finger into a Cauldron of Turtle Soup*

When the puppet king of Chou was reduced to a nonentity, the feudal princes rose to power. Now with the degeneration of these same lords, their authority was usurped by the great officials who served under them. These powerful ministers were in most cases descendants from the same noble stem as the ruler. Some of them might be his brothers and cousins, and others, more distant relatives, but with the same blue blood in their veins. They had their own palatial residences in the capital, with a large retinue of grooms and attendants, horses and chariots. They also had their fiefs in the country protected by walled cities, to which they could retreat in times of trouble. Wielding great sway at court, they could at the height of their power make and unmake a ruler. Whenever the latter became too troublesome or interfering, or whenever they had a personal grudge against him, they did not hesitate to make an end of his life. Punishment for such crimes descended tardily on the culprits, if at all.

There were numerous cases of feudal princes being murdered by their ministers, but perhaps none as ludicrously melodramatic as the story of Duke Ling of Cheng (B.C. 605). He was on his ducal seat barely a few months when a big turtle was presented him by the people of Ch'u. One day, as Tzu-k'ung and Tzu-chia, two ministers, were going to court to have an audience with the duke, Tzu-k'ung's forefinger wiggled. He showed it to Tzu-chia, saying, "On other occasions when my finger moved like this, it was a sure sign that I would taste some rare dish." When they entered the palace, they passed the ducal kitchen, where the cook was cutting up the turtle. They looked at each other and laughed. Thereupon the duke asked the reason, which Tzu-chia told him. Later, when the duke was feasting the great officials on the turtle, he invited to his table Tzu-k'ung, but did not serve him any. At this, Tzu-k'ung was furious. Snatching the opportunity at an unguarded moment, he dipped his finger in the cauldron, tasted the turtle, and ran out. This so enraged the duke that he sought to kill Tzu-k'ung, who in turn became so frightened that he murdered the duke.

But if these were merely incidents, though common enough, a more flagrant example of the usurpation of power by the great officials occurred in Lu, where as early as the middle of the 7th century B.C., exactly a hundred years before the birth of the K'ung child, three aristocratic families, Chi, Meng, and Shu-sun, had monopolized the state affairs. These were founded by the three younger sons of Duke Huan (B.C. 711–694), and, as the nearest in blood to the prince, their chiefs became hereditary ministers during the later reigns. In the course of time they took into their hands the reins of the government, with the duke remaining a mere figurehead. Not satisfied with this encroachment upon ducal authority, they contrived to gain control of the military machinery as well. Up to this time, the armies of any feudal state always belonged to its lord, who alone had the power to appoint their commanders and to call them forth as occasion required. But in 562 B.C., taking advantage of the youth of the reigning duke, the three families of Lu conspired to expand the two armies of the state into three, each family appropriating one of the armies as his own and collecting revenue from the people for its support. They thus apportioned the last ducal prerogative, as it were, into three, with each of them taking one part to himself. Now they were no longer ministers of the state, but its lords, while the reigning duke was henceforth a puppet in their hands.

5. *The Promethean Fire*

If some of the aristocratic houses had, by virtue of sheer luck or ability, climbed up the ladder of success, others suffered a lot entirely different. According to the Chou institution, cadet branches of the noble clan became, at the time they were five generations removed from its progenitor, separated from the main stock and excluded from participation in the ancestral sacrifices. Some of the more ambitious ones established new prosperous houses of their own. But the majority of these families drifted, landless and disinherited, into the vast sea of humanity, where they soon lost their identity and the last vestige of their noble blood. There were also other aristocrats degraded to commonalty or even slavery because of some guilt committed by the head of their clan.[2] At times, when a small fief was conquered and annexed by a powerful neighbor, its lord and officials, thus deprived of their privileges and revenue, were scattered among the masses and soon absorbed by them. Moreover, there was that great class of *shih* on the borderline between aristocracy and commonalty, who, in the course of generations, could easily sink into and merge with the great bulk of good, honest plebeians. In these unstable, transitional times, a great deal of fomentation and upheaval was bound to take place in a fast disintegrating society.

In a certain sense, the dispersion of the disinherited nobles and their amalgamation with the unlettered and underprivileged population was a blessing to the country. It raised the intelligence as well as the standard of living of the common people. Sparks of knowledge began to flicker as the educated descendants of the dispossessed clans, including the historiographers, diviners, and music masters, came into contact with

2. For some very serious crimes, all members of the offender's three clans (those of his father's, mother's and wife's) were annihilated and their ancestral sacrifices discontinued. Many noble families in Tsin, for instance, suffered from this fate. As for common offences, degradation from nobility was the usual punishment.

the common folk. Like the Promethean fire, the light of knowledge was no longer the exclusive possession of the feudal Olym-
pians, but spread among the earthborn, until finally tongues
of flame blazed forth and the torches of learning were kindled
over the length and breadth of the Middle Kingdom.

All these disturbing influences were what the year 551 B.C.
inherited from centuries of strife and change. It was a meager,
unpropitious, but challenging heritage that was bequeathed to
the K'ung child some twenty-five hundred years ago.

CHAPTER THREE

K'ung Ch'iu of Lu

1. *The Commandant of Tsou*

THE REDOUBTABLE COMMANDANT OF TSOU, A SMALL TOWN SOME twenty-five miles from the capital of Lu (Ch'ü-fu), was, according to tradition, an austere man of great prowess and immense stature. He was in 551 B.C. a man in his late sixties; but in his more vigorous days, he had seen great campaigns as one of the commanding officers of the Lu army. For many years past, he had been hailed by his compatriots as a brave warrior, his name appearing twice in the historical records.

Twelve years before (563 B.C.), when he was already middle-aged, Shu-liang Ho of the K'ung clan, for that was the commandant's name, joined from Tsou the grand army of Chinese princes, who periodically gathered to confer against the mighty state of Ch'u. No sooner was the assembly over than its chief general switched the allied hosts to an attack on Pi-yang, a small, but strong viscountcy in the Ch'u orbit of influence. Its defenders, far from being overawed by the spectacle of the besieging allied forces, proceeded to play tricks on the assailants. Purposely leaving open one of the city gates, they suddenly dropped the heavy portcullis on a rash company of allied soldiers who had surged in, thinking that the city would fall an easy prey. The men would have been killed, had it not been for Shu-liang Ho, the hero of our story, who, passing below at this crucial moment, held the portcullis up with his hand, until his comrades-at-arms all made their escape.

Seven years later (556 B.C.), Ho figured again as one of the three officers of Lu, who, with a force of three hundred mail-clad warriors, surprised the invading army of the state of Ch'i in a successful night attack. They then escorted to safety Tsang Ho, a great minister of Lu, who had been besieged by the enemy, and for whose rescue the raiding party had been sent out.

But if the commandant of Tsou was blessed in his old age with memories of such prodigious feats of strength, he was by no means a happy man, so far as his domestic affairs were concerned. This does not mean that he quarrelled with or was divorced from his wife,—though there was such a story—who had borne him nine children, or his concubine, who had a son to her credit. The trouble was that all the children by his first wife were daughters, and the son a cripple; so he was in his declining years still in quest of an amorous adventure that would bring him a male heir to grace the family name of K'ung and to continue unbroken the sacrifices to a long line of distinguished ancestors. How to conduct such a campaign must have presented a great dilemma to the aged commandant who would have felt more at home in a more belligerent type of conquest. Then it happened that on a fortuitous day he had a chance encounter with a young daughter of Yen, barely fifteen; and then on a still more fortuitous day, the twenty-first of the tenth moon,[1] an heir was born to the family of K'ung.

The year was five hundred fifty-one before the Christian era.

1. As a result of the change of the Chinese calendar after the Chou dynasty, the date of K'ung Ch'iu's birth, according to the reckoning of the scholars, fell on the 27th day of the 8th moon. This was further changed to August 27th when China adopted the Western calendar. Today, August 27th is also the Teacher's Day in honor of K'ung Ch'iu.

2. Cheng-Tsai Prays at Ni Ch'iu

The story of Shu-liang Ho's "wild union"[2] was first told in the second century B.C. by Ssu-ma Ch'ien, the father of Chinese history. It must be that such a tradition was current, for the historian saw no objection to using it in his biographical memoirs. But the idea of the illegitimate birth of our future sage,—for here the secret must be told that the K'ung child was none other than the great Chinese sage K'ung Tzu (Master K'ung), whom the Sinologists have dubbed Confucius, but whom we shall call by his true name Ch'iu—must have stung to the quick the sensitive skin of orthodox Chinese respectability. So, as might be expected, there gradually evolved in the course of time a beautifully decent story about the whole affair: the wooing of the old man Ho and the miraculous birth of the child. To these incidents we shall now turn to see how a great historical figure like K'ung Ch'iu suffered from the fate of mummification at the hands of idol-worshippers, until at long last he was laid snugly and eternally in the splendid sarcophagus of myth and legend.

In the course of this metamorphosis, the commandant of Tsou came to be represented as a worthy suitor come a-wooing at the house of Yen. Calling together his three marriageable daughters in a family consultation, father Yen addressed them thus: "Here is the great officer of Tsou, offspring of former sages. He is ten feet tall[3] with prodigious strength. I covet an alliance with him. Though he is austere and old, you need have no misgiving. Which of you three will be his wife?"

2. All the later biographers of K'ung Ch'iu tried to remove this blot on the escutcheon, as they deemed it, by refuting altogether Ssu-ma Ch'ien's account of the "wild union," or by explaining it away in many ingenious ways. Their chief contention was that the word "wild" was in ancient usage an antithesis of *li*, or propriety; and that the union was a "wild" or improper one because of the great disparity in age between the bridegroom and his young bride. You may believe it or not as you please.

3. If we take an ancient Chinese foot as equivalent to 7.4 inches, Ho would still be a "longfellow" of more than six feet tall.

The two elder ones, apparently more worldly-wise, shied away from the idea of marrying a man with one foot already in the grave. So they remained discreetly silent. Cheng-tsai, the youngest, however, dutifully observed, "Why should you ask us, Dad? It's for you to decide."

"Very well," replied her father, "you will do."

So after proper preparations had been made, a wedding was celebrated; and in due time a child was born.

But since the birth of Ch'iu, this extraordinary child, could not be free from a train of auspicious portents and heavenly revelations, the myth-makers again got busy.

As the story goes, Cheng-tsai, the bride of old K'ung, fearing that she might not be able to meet the great expectations of her elderly husband, ascended Ni Ch'iu (the hill Ni) and there prayed for a son.[4] As she trudged up the hill, the leaves of trees and plants stood upright in reverence; and drooped upon her return. On that same night, she dreamed of the Black Emperor's appearing to her in a vision and promising her a son, a sage, who would be born in a hollow mulberry tree. The mulberry tree turned out to be the name of a dry cave on the south side of the hill. There she repaired on the night of her labor, and there the Child was born and "baptized" with the clear, warm waters of a spring that gushed forth from the cave floor at the moment of the Child's birth.

Previously, Cheng-tsai had seen in another wonderful dream five old men, the spirits of the five planets, leading after them the sacred unicorn, a one-horned cow-like creature covered with dragon-scales, to do her homage. Kneeling down before her, the creature cast forth from its mouth a tablet of jade with the following inscription: "The Child of the Essence of Water shall succeed to the decaying Shang and Chou as an Unsceptred King."

4. Another version of the legend represents Cheng-tsai as being accompanied in her devotion by the Commandant. This, in my opinion, spoils a good story.

These anecdotes should suffice for our purpose, though it must be mentioned that there are numerous others, full of sweet voices and subtle fragrance, dragon sprites and female elves. The only point of interest we discover in these stories is that they serve beautifully as a footnote to Ssu-ma Ch'ien's account of the "wild union." As for the prayer episode at Ni Ch'iu, it was very adroitly woven into the legend to give a clue to the two appellations of the Child, who was named Ch'iu[5] and styled Chung-ni (Ni the Younger), in contradistinction to Po-ni (Ni the Elder), the name of his crippled brother.

3. An Illustrious Family-Tree

As a matter of fact, there is no necessity to ennoble the K'ung child with all these stories of a miraculous birth, for his pedigree was illustrious enough. Some of his biographers trace it way back to the Yellow Emperor (flourished B.C. 2700?), the mythical father of the Chinese race. To this claim there can be no dissent, for all Chinese, we know, are descendants of the Yellow Emperor, just as all Jews, and Christians as well, are the offspring of Adam.

Most writers begin K'ung Ch'iu's genealogical table from the first king of the Shang royal house. For our part, we are glad to testify that K'ung Ch'iu came from the great ducal family of the state of Sung, founded by a half-brother of the last king of Shang. One of his ancestors, the famous patriarch Cheng Kao-fu (8th century B.C.), minister to three Sung dukes, was something of a sage, compounded as he was of humility and prudence, for it was said that the greater his promotion, the humbler he became. In an inscription on a bronze tripod he wrote:

5. According to another account, mentioned by Ssu-ma Ch'ien, which is hardly more plausible, the K'ung child received his name Ch'iu from the peculiar shape of his cranium, which, at the time of his birth, looked like a "ch'iu," or a mound with a depression at the top. The real meaning of his name would probably never be known; very likely, there is no significance in it at all.

At the first appointment, I went with bowed head; at the second, with shoulders bent; at the third, with my whole body stooping. Thus I glide by the wall without anybody's daring to insult me. I shall· prepare in this cauldron thick and clear millet, just enough to feed myself.

After Cheng Kao-fu came his son K'ung-fu Chia, founder of the K'ung family. Being now five generations removed from the main ducal stem, and, as was the rule, disinherited from it, he established a clan of his own, adopting as its patronymic his first name K'ung. K'ung-fu, however, did not reap the blessings brought to the family by his father's great virtue. On the contrary, he met with a tragic death because of his wife's beauty. It happened like this: When K'ung-fu was minister of war, he had as his superior Hua Tu, the chief minister. One day Hua happened to meet K'ung-fu's wife on the street, and was so dazzled by her charm that he could not take his eyes off her, all the while exclaiming to himself, "How perfectly beautiful; how perfectly lovely!" The next year (710 B.C.), Hua attacked the family of K'ung, killed K'ung-fu, and ran off with his wife. But she was so grieved and so resentful against her captor that on her way to Hua's house, she strangled herself with a girdle. This, however, did not deter Hua in his murderous orgy, for fear of princely justice upon this atrocious deed now led him to murder the duke and plant a younger puppet in his seat.

After that a great enmity arose between the families of K'ung and Hua until Fang Shu, K'ung-fu's great-grandson, withdrew from Sung to the neighboring state of Lu to avoid further persecution by his more powerful enemy. He was given a fief at Fang, where the K'ungs established themselves. Two generations later, Shu-liang Ho (B.C. 625–549?) settled at Tsou as its commandant, and there the child Ch'iu was born.

4. *A Political Interlude—The World's First Peace Conference*

It is almost impossible to believe that there could develop in this age of political vicissitudes the beginning of a momentous event that flowered, when K'ung Ch'iu was five years old, into the world's first peace conference. It was a full-fledged one, at that, called to order in the capital of Sung and attended by princes and great ministers of twelve Chinese states, including practically all those that had figured in the contentious history of the period. The meeting was held without the grace of the reigning king of Chou. This, however, does not mean that he was niggardly in giving his royal sanction to such a highly laudable gesture of peace. On the contrary, it indicates that by this time the Chou sovereign had been altogether eliminated from the political scene, and his presence or approval was no longer craved by the independent feudal states.

The chief promoter of the peace assembly was Hsiang Shu, a minister of Sung and a veteran diplomat. At this great distance we have no means of discovering the ulterior motive that led him to initiate the move. But the desire to stop the constant warfare among the states must have been uppermost in his mind when Hsiang Shu volunteered as the first peacemaker in history. The Middle Kingdom was then divided into two camps with Tsin and Ch'u respectively as their standardbearers. By a stroke of fortune, Hsiang Shu was on friendly terms with the great ministers of both states. Moreover, the Chinese people had grown tired of bootless bloodshed after centuries of intermittent warfare, and though none of the rulers really wanted peace, the word cast such a magic spell that it disarmed all opposition in a war-weary world. So when Hsiang Shu broached the subject to the great states, they all endorsed his project, though at first with a good deal of misgiving.

After some adroit machination and statesmanship, much persuading and convincing, Hsiang Shu succeeded at length in bringing together the plenipotentiaries of all the important Chinese states in an unparalleled and, as we shall later see, not entirely futile attempt at peace. The meeting was held at Sung in the fifth month of the year 546 B.C. At the outset, jealousy and suspicion stalked among the assembled nations, especially between Tsin and Ch'u. The emissaries, with their numerous attendants and assistants, pitched camp outside the Sung capital, but a wide fence was used to separate Tsin and Ch'u. The men of Ch'u, moreover, went to the assembly wearing armor under their outer garments, thus unnerving the other peace delegates. Then there was a verbal bout between Tsin and Ch'u over the question of precedence, until it was finally agreed to give it to Ch'u, but with the understanding that Tsin's name would appear first in the written text.

Three days later, outside the western gate of the Sung capital, Duke P'ing of Sung and the ministers of all the other states present swore to an epoch-making covenant.

If we are to conclude from the mutually suspicious attitude of Tsin and Ch'u at this meeting that the treaty was doomed to be a mere scrap of paper to last, at most, a few years, we are sadly mistaken. The Chinese states of those days, it seems, kept their word much more faithfully than do nations today. Minor skirmishes there were after the conference, but no major war was waged among the big states for almost half a century. As a matter of fact, peace endured in Sung for fifty-one years, in Ts'ao for forty-eight years, in Wey and Cheng for forty-three and forty-two years respectively. In the state of Lu, where K'ung Ch'iu was born, there was peace for forty-three years, until it was broken by an invasion of Ch'i in 503 B.C. Though internal dissensions were a-plenty, with stewards rebelling against their minister-masters, and high officials putting the duke into exile, the people of Lu were happily spared from those disastrous and exhaustive interstate wars. So, thanks to the pioneer efforts of Hsiang Shu, the child of K'ung was lucky to live in a period when there was comparative quiet at home and abroad.

5. *Ch'iu Seeks and Finds His Father's Grave*

Practically nothing is known about K'ung Ch'iu's childhood except that the redoubtable commandant of Tsou died when Ch'iu was only three years old. At six he was credited with showing a precocious interest in the observance of *li*, posturizing and mimicking the ancient rites, while tinkering with makeshift sacrificial vessels and altar tables. Tradition also assigns his first schooling at the age of seven, which is probable, but the details of his education, conflicting and unreliable as they are, must not detain us here. We need only to observe in passing that the young Ch'iu was being initiated into a career entirely different from that of his soldierly father, and very likely, the influence came from his mother's side.

About the lady herself we know very little, besides the stories already told of her filial obedience that culminated in her marriage, and her ardent prayer at Ni Ch'iu, which was happily answered. A deep mystery seems to enshroud her relation with the other members of the commandant's family. From this and the other meager evidences we are able to gather, it seems that she did not get along very well with them, considering especially that her nine stepdaughters were all much older than she. It is odd that Shu-liang Ho was buried, not in Tsou, where his young wife and son were and where, presumably, he died, but in Fang, the first home of the K'ung family in Lu. It is even stranger that the child Ch'iu should have grown up, as he did, without being told of the whereabouts of his father's grave, for Cheng-tsai kept it a secret from him to the end of her life. Apparently he had no means of communicating with or soliciting information from his elder brother and sisters who should have known. Are we then not justified in supposing that something must have gone wrong in the K'ung family, and that it must have been extremely uncomfortable for the ceremonial-minded boy to be kept in sad ignorance of his father's resting place, especially in a society in which ancestor worship was so important?

We have no record of the exact date when the family moved from Tsou to its new home in the Lu capital. But it is quite likely that the move was made not long after Ho's death. The mother and son must have settled there for a number of years before Ch'iu, now a young man of nineteen (533 B.C.), took to wife a daughter of the Chien-kuan clan from the state of Sung. About the bride and her family nothing is known; neither are we any wiser about the compatibility of the newly wedded couple. But the birth of a son the next year was the occasion of great joy in the K'ung family, climaxed by the ceremonial presentation of a carp from the reigning duke of Lu. To perpetuate this honor in the family history, the infant was given the name Li (Carp), and later was called Po-yü (Fish, the Elder).

As the son of a military officer, descended from aristocratic stock, K'ung Ch'iu belonged to that great class of lesser nobility known as *shih*. It is not clear when he came to his patrimony, or whether there was any at all. Apparently, the family was, in spite of its aristocratic connections, in straitened circumstances, and the young man had to start life the hard way by filling some minor public posts to support his growing family. True to the old tradition of *shih*, he was keeper of the granary and later supervisor of the flocks and herds.[6] In both positions he was most punctilious, and soon became noted for the fairness of his measure, the exactness of his calculation, and the

6. It is a matter of controversy whether K'ung Ch'iu was in the employment of the duke (according to Meng K'o) or the Chi clan (according to Ssu-ma Ch'ien), whose head was the chief minister in Lu. Probably it amounts to the same thing as any state appointment had to come from the all-powerful minister, who actually ran the ducal government.

meticulous care he gave to the multiplication and fattening of the cattle and sheep. Though mean positions, they gave the future philosopher an understanding of life and its vicissitudes. "When I was young," he told his pupils, "my condition was lowly, and, for this reason, I acquired ability in many things."

The death of his mother (528 B.C.) and the subsequent three years' mourning put an end to Ch'iu's public duties. During this period of bereavement, he must have led, in accordance with the ritualistic observances of the time, a life of seclusion and dejection, refraining from sensual indulgences and activities, such as drinking, hunting, fishing, music, and visits to friends. As a filial son, he was also anxious to place his mother's remains beside his father's, so that the two might rest together in eternal peace. Giving his mother a temporary interment off the Street of Five Fathers in the capital of Lu,[7] he started on a long and arduous quest for his father's grave until he finally learned of its location from an old woman of Tsou. Then taking along his mother's coffin, he buried his parents together at Fang near the ancestral house of the K'ungs in Lu.

One of the Chou innovations in matters of burial was the rearing of a mound over the grave to serve as a landmark. Following the usual custom, Ch'iu made a knoll four feet high over his parents' burial ground, saying to himself, "In olden

7. I can find no support for Legge's statement, followed by all subsequent writers of K'ung Ch'iu's life, that Ho's coffin was deposited "off the Road of The Five Fathers, in the vicinity of Tsow." (Legge, *Chinese Classics*, I, "Prolegomena," p. 61.) All evidences from the *Book of Rites* (Legge, *Li Ki, in the Sacred Books of the East*, XXVII, 123–5) to the "Life of K'ung-tzu" by Ssu-ma Ch'ien (Richard Wilhelm, *Confucius and Confucianism*, p. 4) clearly indicate that K'ung Ch'iu's father was buried at Fang, his ancestral home at Lu. The Road of the Five Fathers, moreover, was not in the vicinity of Tsou, but it was a main thoroughfare in Ch'ü-fu, the capital of Lu. From the *Tso's Commentary*, we also know that the street was an important meeting place of the Lu people, where the imprecatory sentences of the covenants made by the aristocrats were usually proclaimed. (See, for instance, Legge, *Chinese Classics*, V, 450, 452.)

times no such memorials were raised, but being a man of the east and west, of the south and north, I shall not leave the grave without a marker." But as soon as he left, a torrential rain swept the.hillock away. When this was reported to him, he burst into tears, exclaiming, "The ancients did not have such mounds!"

6. *He Dreams of Duke Chou*

Little is known of what K'ung Ch'iu did during the three years in which he mourned his mother's death, as was decorous for a gentleman of propriety. Neither is it clear what position he took up immediately after the period of mourning was over. But it may be surmised that in these quiet, uneventful years of forced inaction, he must have given his future calling long and serious thought, now that he was on the threshold of his manly life. The world looked temptingly bright and good, full of latent possibilities and undiscovered resources,— and it all was his to explore and conquer. But what could he do? What aspiration was agitating his breast? For what strange harbor was his ship of life bound? And weren't there divine voices calling to him and urging him on to the mission that he was decreed to undertake?

Happily for the young man, he had long days and months to ponder over these great and unfathomable questions. It was certain that he would not follow in the footsteps of his father to become a military man. To be sure, he was familiar with the warlike arts of chariot-driving and archery, but he had learned these more as a part of his aristocratic education, indigent and dispossessed a noble as he was, than as a preparation for a martial career. On the other hand, there was one subject by which he was particularly intrigued. From childhood, he had been fascinated by the performance of rituals, and since the age of fifteen, had also been particularly interested in learning. To the scholarly scion of the K'ung family, therefore, the polar world of Chou culture, with its music and ceremony, history and poetry, must have been irresistibly attractive and alluring.

Gradually, the solution to the riddle of his future began to emerge and later to crystallize in his mind. In this crucial period of his life, young Ch'iu, after having engaged in long moments of profound meditation, now dreamed that he saw the renowned Duke of Chou, that great progenitor of the ducal house of Lu, who was responsible, as we have seen, for the establishment of the Chou kingdom with its ceremonial and cultural institutions. He remembered that because of this heritage, Lu was always regarded as a center of learning and ceremony, and as such, was respected by the other feudal states. It is hard to see how K'ung Ch'iu, who was born and bred in Lu, could very well escape being influenced by the intellectual atmosphere that enveloped him. Others might, but certainly not the young man who had in him the blood of the humble sage Cheng Kao-fu. In his old age K'ung Ch'iu used to refer to this idealistic period of his life by exclaiming, "How great is my decay! For a long time now I have not dreamed, as I was wont to do, that I saw the Duke of Chou." We are inclined to believe that this dream must have been repeated over a long period of time and must have originated in the days when he was earnestly mapping out a worthy career for himself. Thus, inspired and goaded on by such an uplifting vision, he had no other choice but to take up the torch left by the Duke of Chou and to pass it on to posterity. A momentous decision had been made. If it was not his lot to emulate the illustrious Duke of Chou as a ruler of men, though this was his ultimate aim, he could be at least a scholar, a teacher of men.

But how was he to equip himself for this noble calling? In what branch of polite learning should he specialize and instruct his pupils? To answer these questions, we must turn to the early days of feudal society, when, it will be remembered, the alpha and omega of aristocratic culture was *li*, a summation of the rites and etiquette of the times, derived from religious practices, and having music as its accompaniment. As noted above, *li* was also the acme of nobility, in which the youngest lordlings were initiated by their tutors. These, you will recall, might have been originally music masters[8] and masters of ceremony, who played an important part in the ritualistic performances of the state. Under these circumstances, it was natural for the youthful K'ung to educate himself in the arts of music and rites as the starting point of his teaching career. This apparently he did. Besides being prodigious in the mimicry of ceremonials as a child, he also had the reputation of poking his nose into every object of curiosity in the grand temple of Lu. He was truly a man of feudal tradition.

There are two specific records of his indefatigable search for the light of knowledge. In the autumn of 525 B.C., when K'ung Ch'iu was twenty-seven, and his period of mourning just over, the viscount of T'an paid a friendly call at the court of Lu. In an entertainment given him by the duke, the visiting ruler made a great impression on the host and his ministers by discoursing learnedly on the strange ways in which the officials of the prehistoric dynasties were designated. He told how the Yellow Emperor, who came to the throne with the omen of a cloud, named his officials after the various nebulous formations, and how other emperors of antiquity had *fire* ministers, *water* ministers, and *dragon* ministers. As for his progenitor Shao Hao (flourished B.C. 2600?) the eldest son of the Yellow Emperor, he designated his officials as members of the feathered kingdom to honor the miraculous *feng huang* (phoenix

8. As pointed out in the first chapter, music masters were also originally tutors, whose names were generally prefixed with the word "shih," meaning master or teacher.

or vermilion bird) which appeared at the time he ascended the throne. Thus in the court of Shao Hao, to whom the viscount traced his lineage some twenty centuries before, there was a veritable parliament of fowls, with all the great officials called by the names of Sparrow and Shrike, Pheasant and Phoenix, Turtledove and Pigeon, and what not. This was a most fascinating discourse replete with antiquarian lore, and K'ung Ch'iu, who was fortunate in having obtained an interview with the viscount, learned much from him.

Sometime later, in his twenty-ninth year (523 B.C.), he went to study music under Hsiang, master of the musical stone at the court of Lu.[9] Ch'iu became so proficient in his performance on the zither that he won the teacher's great admiration. Once, as the story goes, he was given a piece of music without being told the name of the composer. After many days of practice and concentration upon the mood and theme of the composition, he went back to the master: "I have at last found him out! He is dark, tall and large. His eyes are those of a ram looking into the distance; his mind is that of a king of the four quarters of the earth. If it was not King Wen, who else could have composed anything like this?" Hearing these words, Master Hsiang rose from the mat, bowed twice, and exclaimed, "You are certainly a genius!"

7. The Deathbed Will of Minister Meng

The time was now ripe for K'ung Ch'iu's launching out into that great and as yet unexplored profession known as teaching. In his humble schoolroom in Lu, there now gathered a group

9. There being no means of verifying or refuting this traditional date of K'ung Ch'iu's learning music from Master Hsiang, the best we can do is to follow it. Hsiang was said to be the music master of either Tsin or Wey. But there is no record of K'ung Ch'iu's going to either of the two states at this period of his life, and it is unlikely that he ever took such a trip. Therefore I follow Legge in identifying Master Hsiang with another of his namesake, the master of musical stone at the court of Lu. (See the Analects, XVIII, 9; in Legge, Chinese Classics, I, 202.)

of aspiring young men of all descriptions, who came to him, with a bundle of dried meat for tuition, to be instructed in the highly commendable and useful knowledge of *li* and its accompanying arts. As such it was a great innovation in the Chou world. To be sure, in ancient times, all branches of learning were in the official custody of hereditary scholars attached to the prince's court. But never before the sixth century B.C. had a private individual formally engaged in public teaching. If there had been a private teacher before this time, history would certainly have given him a welcome account. But since no such name has been discovered so far, K'ung Ch'iu has the distinction, and a great distinction too, of being the first teacher in the intellectual history of China.

According to tradition, he commenced teaching at the age of twenty-two.[10] But this date is highly improbable, not only because he was then too young for such a dignified and novel profession, but also because he was most probably still engaged in his public work as Overseer of the Granary, and later, of the Fields,—both positions being incompatible with teaching. Furthermore, he had to have time to study before he could teach, since his early schooling was inadequate for such a great undertaking. Hence it is more likely that he made up his mind to pursue this noble and challenging calling at the time of his bereavement, and that he prepared himself for it in the following years by seizing every opportunity of learning that came his way. It would be reasonable to suppose, therefore, that his teaching career began in or a little before his thirtieth year, when we learn definitely from an historical record the name of one of his first pupils, Chin Chang.[11] It was also in this year, according to his own testimony, that he had established himself.

10. Legge, for instance, wrote: "In his twenty-second year, Confucius commenced his labours as a public teacher." (*Chinese Classics*, I, "Prolegomena," p. 61.)

11. Chin Chang was mentioned as K'ung Ch'iu's pupil in the *Tso's Commentary* under that year. (Legge, *Chinese Classics*, V, 682.)

It took only four years more for him to become well-known among the intellectual circles of Lu as a reputed master of ceremonials, as shown in the following story:

In the second month of 518 B.C., Meng Hsi-tzu, head of one of the three noble families in Lu, was lying on his deathbed.[12] He was a man of great prominence, having served for many years as minister to the reigning duke, and as an emissary on several diplomatic missions. Previously, however, there had been a blot on the Meng escutcheon. Early in 535 B.C., Hsi-tzu had accompanied his prince as a ceremonial assistant on a trip to Ch'u. With all the feudatories now on friendly terms with one another as a result of Hsiang Shu's peace movement, the duke of Lu was invited along with the other rulers to attend a dedicatory feast given by the viscount (or king, as he styled himself) of Ch'u on the completion of his splendid pleasure tower. The distinguished Lu visitors were first greeted by the earl of Cheng, as they passed by his domain, and later by the viscount of Ch'u on the suburbs of his great state. But on both occasions, Minister Meng sadly failed to conduct the ceremonial observances suitable to the meeting of feudal princes. As great a personal loss of face as it was, it was still greater disgrace to his state which had long been noted for its ceremony and etiquette. So immediately after his return from Ch'u, to mend his shortcoming, Meng set about learning the rites from recognized masters of ceremony, until he himself became a connoisseur of *li*. Now as he was breathing his last, he called to-

12. The deathbed will of Minister Meng was entered in the *Tso's Commentary* under the 7th year of Duke Chao of Lu (B.C. 535) immediately after the story of Meng's failure to conduct the ceremonials at Cheng and Ch'u (Legge, *Chinese Classics*, V, 616), but actually the death of Minister Meng occurred in the 24th year of Duke Chao (B.C. 518) as found in a separate entry under that year in the *Tso's Commentary*. (Legge, *Chinese Classics*, V, 702.) Ssu-ma Ch'ien, however, failed to notice the entry of Meng's death in *Tso*, and left the wrong impression, followed by later Chinese biographers, of Meng's leaving his two sons in Master K'ung's charge in 535 B.C., when the latter was only in his seventeenth year. (See P. W. Yetts, *The Legend of Confucius*, Appendix II, p. 38.)

gether his two sons Yueh and Ho-chi,[13] as well as the heads of his family, and said to them: "A knowledge of *li* is the stem of man, without which he cannot stand firm. I have heard that there is a rising man of great intelligence, called K'ung Ch'iu, a descendant of sage-rulers." Then after enumerating the several virtues of K'ung's forebears, he continued, addressing the elders of his clan:

Tsang-sun Ho[14] used to say, "If a man of brilliant capacity does not become distinguished in his lifetime, there is bound to be among his posterity someone of vast intelligence." This is now verified in the person of K'ung Ch'iu. If I should die, you must put Yueh and Ho-chi under his charge to learn the ceremonials from him, in order that they may become properly established in their positions.

The death of Minister Meng proved to be the making of K'ung Ch'iu. At the outset of his teaching career, there might have been moments of misgiving, hesitancy, and frustration, but he was able to stand firm in his convictions. And now in his thirty-fourth year, with the two young scions of the great Meng family entering the portals of his schoolroom, his reputation as a full-fledged tutor increased. Students continued to flock around him, contributing more and more to his fame and resources. What he needed now was to have more inspiration for his teaching, to broaden the vista of his learning, and to gain a first-hand knowledge of Chou culture by drinking directly from its fountainhead. A tour of the Chou capital at Lo must have been for years the one great yearning of schoolmaster K'ung. Happily for him, the chances of its fulfilment were no longer remote.

13. There is an interesting story of the birth of the twins Yueh and Ho-chi in the *Tso's Commentary* under the 11th year of Duke Chao (B.C. 531). (See Legge, *Chinese Classics,* V, 634.)

After Hsi-tzu's death, Ho-chi (Meng I-tzu) succeeded his father as head of the family and minister of the state.

14. Tsang-sun Ho, or Tsang Ho, was the same minister of Lu rescued from the Ch'i army by Shu-liang Ho, K'ung Ch'iu's father.

CHAPTER FOUR

The Man of Ceremony

1. *A Grand Tour of Lo, the Royal Capital*

THE STORY OF K'UNG CH'IU'S TRIP TO THE ROYAL CAPITAL AND
his meeting with Lao Tan, popularly known as Lao Tzu, has
long been a matter of academic dispute. There is a tendency
among Chinese scholars today to deny the existence of such a
person as Lao Tan, the reputed founder of the Taoist school of
philosophy, and to discredit altogether the episode of K'ung
Ch'iu's visit to Lo.[1] To us, however, their arguments seem to
be more hair-splitting than convincing. Some minor inaccura-
cies and inconsistencies there are in the traditional records,
but these need not deter us from believing in the authenticity
of the story itself, which, in truth, is too good to be untrue.
Moreover, it is inconceivable that K'ung Ch'iu, who grew up
to be the greatest spokesman of Chou, should thus be deprived
of an opportunity to enter into the sanctum sanctorum of its
learning, and to explore therein its magnificent treasure-trove
as he is said to have done.

The main purpose of K'ung Ch'iu's visit was to study, or as
the Chinese put it, to inquire about the rites. Chou had long

1. Ch'ien Mu, for instance, wrote: "As for the story of K'ung Ch'iu's inquiring
about the rites from Lao Tan, there is not only difficulty in fixing the date, but
also uncertainty about the place of their meeting. Indeed, there is no proof of
the existence of such a person (as Lao Tan), and little basis for the whole episode." (Ch'ien Mu, *An Interlinking Chronology of the Ante-Ch'in Philosophers,*
Shanghai, 1935, p. 8.)

47

been politically inactive, but in matters of culture, it was still a source of the greatest inspiration to all students of antiquity. Its glory had faded, to be sure, but traces of its splendor were still discernible in the august capital at Lo. So to this city of his dream, built by the Duke of Chou, schoolman K'ung now made preparations to go. Tradition has it that Yueh, better known as Nan-kung Ching-shu, accompanied the Master on his trip,[2] having first obtained for him the duke's permission as well as the ducal present of a two-horsed carriage with a coach-man-page. Equipped in such a noble style, K'ung Ch'iu set out on his grand journey. It was probably the most exciting, if not the happiest, moment of his life, as he toured the two hundred fifty miles from Lu to Chou in the year 518 B.C.[3]

After having arrived at Lo, the royal city, tourist K'ung set about eagerly on many sight-seeing trips. The splendid architecture of his dream-city was a revelation to him. Here were the sacred grounds set apart for the regal sacrifices to Heaven and Earth; there were the court precincts, in which had lived a long line of kings, descended from the illustrious Wen and Wu. In the hall of the Grand Temple, where the ancestral rites of the sovereign house were held, K'ung Ch'iu, the moralist, was intrigued with the gold statue[4] of a man with three clasps on his mouth, and on his back a homily, which began: "Be careful of your speech. Don't talk too much, for much talk leads to calamity."

2. The objection is that Nan-kung Ching-shu (Yueh) should be mourning his father's death at home, instead of taking a trip to Lo. But there was nothing to prevent Master K'ung from going on the journey.

3. According to a record in the *Book of Rites*, K'ung Ch'iu was assisting Lao Tan in a funeral ceremony when the sun eclipsed. (Legge, *Li Ki*, in the *Sacred Books of the East*, XXVII, 339.) This placed K'ung Ch'iu's visit to Lo and his meeting with Lao Tan in the 24th year of Duke Chao (B.C. 518), when on the 1st day of the 5th month that year, such an eclipse did occur. (Legge, *Chinese Classics*, V, 702.)

4. The statue was probably a bronze one, all metals being indiscriminately called gold in that period.

The most inspiring sight, however, was the Hall of Light,[5] a huge structure for the official reception of the visiting feudal lords, on the walls of which were painted pictures of the ancient sovereigns. Here in this royal portrait gallery, K'ung Ch'iu stood silent and reverent, gazing long and intently, for there among the many portraits was that of the man who had appeared to him in his dream. It was the Duke of Chou, in the full splendor of his court dress, seated, and holding his nephew, the young king Cheng (B.C. 1115–1079), on his knees, ready to give audience to the assembled feudal princes. Deeply moved, the schoolmaster turned to his followers, exclaiming: "Here you see why Chou was so great! As we use a mirror to reflect the form of things, so we look into the past to understand the future."

Besides sight-seeing, K'ung Ch'iu was also busily engaged in paying visits to the intellectual celebrities of the capital. Rites and music being his main inquiry, he interviewed Ch'ang Hung, the famous musician, and Lao Tan, curator of the royal archives. The former, greatly impressed by the accomplished schoolman from Lu, was unstinted in his praise: "When he speaks, he extols the ancient kings. He moves along the path of humility and courtesy. He has heard of every subject, and retains with a strong memory. His knowledge of things seems inexhaustible. Have we not in him the promise of a sage?" But the more skeptical Lao Tan dismissed K'ung Ch'iu with the following parting advice:

I have heard that the rich and great make valuable farewell gifts, but the good present people with advice. I, who am neither rich nor great, but who venture to call myself a good man, shall set you on your way with these words: "A brilliant and discerning man is nigh to death, for he is apt to court danger by criticizing

5. The Hall of Light, originally the ancestral temple of the Chou sovereigns, was also apparently used as a reception hall. It was here, as we shall soon see, that the Duke of Chou gave audience to the feudal princes during his regency for his young nephew, King Cheng, who succeeded King Wu on the throne.

other people; a man with a vast understanding in many fields imperils himself, because he likes to expose others' frailties. He who is a son has nothing to call his own; nor has he who is a minister at court."

Another account represents the imperial curator as giving the zealous inquirer into *li* a practical lesson on the art of wise living:

Those whom you talk about are dead, and their bones are moldered away; only their words remain. When a superior man gets his chance, he mounts aloft; but when time is against him, he moves as if his feet were entangled. I have heard that a good merchant stores away his treasures as if he were destitute, and that the princely gentleman who prospers in virtue appears as if he were stupid. Get rid of your supercilious airs and inordinate passions, your insinuating manners and lustful ambitions. That's all I have to tell you.

Instead of being ruffled by this honest, blunt advice, K'ung Ch'iu, on the contrary, praised the elder philosopher to his pupils in these flamboyant words:

Birds I know can fly, fishes can swim, and animals can run. But as for the dragon, I can't tell how it mounts on the winds and clouds to rise to heaven. Lao Tzu, isn't he indeed such a dragon!

We have no way of either verifying or denying the genuineness of these speeches, unless we were to call the interlocutors from their grave. But there is nothing implausible about the whole affair. K'ung Ch'iu was then in his thirty-fourth year, while Lao Tan must have been reputedly quite advanced in age. Being the older and wiser of the two, he was entitled to a patronizing attitude towards his admiring visitor. Moreover, the good grace with which the younger man acknowledged these words of mellow wisdom bespeaks of his humility and affability that are the hallmarks of a sage.

In any case, there can be little doubt that the trip to Lo was a major event in the life of K'ung Ch'iu. It completed his education as a teacher, it enriched his knowledge of *li*, it matured his outlook and widened his experience of life, it led him to a deeper understanding of the cultural past, it opened up new vistas for his future pursuit, while at the same time it convinced him of the greatness and nobleness of the mission he had undertaken. By worldly standards, he had grown in stature and status. From now on he would no longer be a mere K'ung Ch'iu of Lu, but the renowned Master K'ung of history.

2. *An Historical Cock-Fight*

The year after K'ung Ch'iu's trip to the royal capital, portentous events happened in the state of Lu. There had been drought for two successive years and it continued in severity in the autumn of 517 B.C., notwithstanding repeated sacrifices to the god of rain. The myna grackles, birds previously unknown in that part of the country, came to nest on the trees in the capital. By means of these unusual occurrences, Heaven and Nature seemed to forewarn the state of its impending disaster, which finally came as an aftermath of a cock-fight.

At the time, the government of Lu, as mentioned above, was in the hands of its three noble families, Chi, Meng, and Shu-sun, whose heads filled respectively the three chief ministerial posts of Instruction, Works, and War. The Chi clan, the most powerful of the three, had had control of the state for several generations, and its present chief P'ing-tzu, having been prime minister for the last eighteen years, wielded great authority at court. In fact he became so presumptuous that he usurped not only the ducal, but also the royal, prerogative by employing eight rows of eight dancers each in pantomimic performances in the front courtyard of his mansion, the regular number of rows being four for a great minister. Thus it happened that at the time *ti,* the great quinquennial sacrifice, was about to be offered in the temple of Hsiang, deceased father of the reigning duke Chao, the officer-in-charge found himself short of dancers, with only sixteen of the regular performers left in the ducal household, the others having gone to dance in the Chi family. When this infringement was made public, the great officers murmured and complained.

The long enmity between P'ing-tzu and the court faction surrounding Duke Chao, who all resented minister Chi's domineering attitude, broke wide open. As early as 530 B.C., the twelfth year of the duke, an abortive attempt by some political agitators had been made to oust P'ing-tzu from Lu. Now the situation was further aggravated by a private feud between the Chi and Hou families over an ignoble cock-fight. In this historic battle of the birds, the Chi clan played unfair by sheathing the head of their prize cock, but the Hous retaliated by arming theirs with a metal spur.[6] The uproar that followed this unsportsmanlike game must have been terrific, for P'ing-tzu, enraged at his adversary, retaliated by building by force a wing of his palatial mansion on the estate of the Hou family, while at the same time publicly reprimanding its head for the fracas.

Grievances against P'ing-tzu mounted. Joined by malcontents from inside the Chi clan itself, the enemies of P'ing-tzu plotted his overthrow and succeeded in gaining Duke Chao's sympathetic, though timorous, ear. Things now came to such a pass that the arrow of Nemesis went whizzing out of the overstrung bow with a deadly twang. Led personally by the duke, the insurgent party made an attack on the Chi residence and,

6. Carl Crow gives a dramatic, but inaccurate, account of the story as follows: "On this occasion of the historical contest, Baron P'ing of Chi concealed freshly grounded mustard in the feathers of his bird disposing the irritant so as partially to blind the other bird when he buried his beak in the neck of his adversary preparatory to delivering the fatal thrust with his spurs." (*Master Kung*, p. 115.) The mustard idea seems to have come from a misrendering of the Chinese word *chieh*, meaning armor or to armor, as another word of the same sound meaning mustard plant.

entering its gate, stormed the quarters of P'ing-tzu, as he fled hurriedly up the turreted terrace of his stronghold. But at this juncture, while the duke's men were laying down their "buff-coats" to recuperate for a renewed assault, the retainers of Shu-sun, waving aloft the clan insignia, swarmed to the rescue of the beleaguered, their slogan being that there would be no Shu-sun without the Chi. In the meantime, the Meng followers, sighting at a distance the Shu-sun flags at the city's north-west corner, joined forces with them to attack the ducal party, which they together easily put to rout.

After holding a brief consultation with his supporters at the family cemetery, the duke decided on flight. He first went to Ch'i, and three years later, to Kan-hou in Tsin. In both states he received a lukewarm reception, and after several futile attempts at restoration, died in the seventh year of his exile (510 B.C.) at Kan-hou. A ditty of the times, recalling the unusual appearance of the mynas on the trees of Lu, runs as follows:

> Here are the grackles apace;
> The duke flies in disgrace!
> Look at the grackles' wings;
> To the wilds the duke flings! . . .
> In Kan-hou he is low,
> Wants coats and trousers now.
> Behold the grackle's nest!
> Far off the duke doth rest. . . .
> O the grackles so strange!
> Their songs to weeping change.

3. The Tyrant or the Tiger?

While disorder was running riot in the capital of Lu, with the followers of the three noble families engaging the duke's men in a bloody melee, Master K'ung, who had just shaken himself free from the dust of his trip to Lo the year before, quietly pursued his independent, respectable calling as a

teacher of youth. Newly baptized in the fountain of Chou culture, he had already identified himself with the great feudal
traditions handed down by the sagacious Duke; and nothing
could be more distasteful to him than to see ministers treading
on the toes of the reigning prince, thereby violating the code
of *li* that made strict distinctions between the lord and his subjects. It was in this spirit that he had condemned the Chi's presumptuous use of the eight-rowed pantomimic dancers, nothing being more unbearable, according to him, than this and
similar acts of arrogance. But now for the ministers to rise in
arms against the duke and put him to flight must have come
as a terrific shock to the orthodox schoolmaster.

Being independent of the court faction, Master K'ung was
not forced to flee from his state. But as an uncompromising
loyalist, he chose for himself the path of voluntary exile.
Deeply distracted and full of righteous indignation, he hastened to Ch'i in the wake of the ducal party. It was a gesture of
protest, however vain and feeble, against the unruly events of
the day; it was a show of respect and sympathy for the duke;
and it was also a form of propriety for a faithful subject to
condole with his prince by sharing in his misfortune. And had
he not been honored only recently by the lordly gift of a carriage and horses? This favor he could not afford to ignore.
Duke Chao, moreover, was known to have great respect for
ceremonies, and for this reason there might have been, con-
sciously or unconsciously, a bond of attachment between him
and the distinguished scholar of his state.

Nevertheless, Master K'ung did not join the duke's retinue
at the border town of Ch'i; instead, he went straight to its
capital at Lin-tzu, some hundred miles north of Lu. According
to one account, Ching (B.C. 547–490), the reigning duke of
Ch'i, while on a hunting trip to the suburb of Lu five years
before, had paid a friendly visit to that state to inquire about

the rites, and there had engaged Master K'ung in a private discourse on the differences between kingship and hegemony. But the episode itself is open to doubt, there being no record of such a regal visit in the annals of Lu. Moreover, the tenor of Master K'ung's speech, as reported by the same source, is more in keeping with the prevalent view of a later age, when government by kingly sway was a favorite topic of the scholars. Furthermore, it is unlikely that K'ung Ch'iu, who was just commencing his teaching career at that time, should loom so large among his fellows as to attract the attention of a visiting prince.

Even disregarding this highly dubious episode of his earlier meeting with Duke Ching, it is quite conceivable why K'ung Ch'iu should have chosen Ch'i as a temporary haven from the political storms in his own state. Besides being a place of refuge for the fugitive Chao, Ch'i was also the only big state near by which could exercise, if it wished, considerable influence on the affairs of Lu. K'ung Ch'iu was then in the prime of his manhood, and restless thoughts by no means pedagogical must have been fomenting in his mind, impelling and instigating him to play the perilous game of politics, which indeed was not entirely alien to his inclination. The roving, adventurous blood of the brave commandant of Tsou was in his veins,—his ambitions, however, were not military, but political.

Before we proceed to narrate K'ung Ch'iu's visit to Ch'i, let us pause for a little wayside story beautifully illustrative of his method of teaching. As the Lu travelers were leaving the borders of their native land for the strange country of Ch'i, the story says that they came face to face with the grandeur of Mount T'ai, one of the five sacred mountains of China from time immemorial. Standing rapt in breathless admiration of the majestic scene before them, they were suddenly struck by a woman's heart-rending cries that pierced the immense wilds. Bending forward to the cross-bar of his travelling cart, Master K'ung listened. It was unmistakably the cries of an anguished woman that rent the air. He hastened forward, and saw a peasant woman weeping bitterly by a grave. Without dismounting, he sent Tzu-lu, a young swashbuckler who had recently joined his scholarly band, to ask for the cause of her grief.

"Hi! You weep as if you had suffered from great sorrows," inquired the dashing young man.

"It is so," answered the distressed female. "First my father-in-law was killed here by a tiger; then my husband met the same fate; and now death has come to my son!"

"But why don't you leave this place?"

"There is no oppressive government here," was the reply.

Hearing this, the Master turned to his followers and said, "My children, remember this: An oppressive government is fiercer than a tiger!"

4. *Eight Sphinx-Like Words*

Whatever might be his other motives, it is undeniable that K'ung Ch'iu's visit to Ch'i was promoted by the ambition to gain access to the ear of its reigning duke Ching, and thereby to ingratiate himself in the latter's favor. Perhaps he even entertained the wild hope of bringing about the restoration of the exiled Chao through his connections and ministrations in Ch'i. With this in view, he obtained, immediately upon his arrival there, an introduction to Kao Chao-tzu, a court favorite, in whose service he established himself, thus becoming a visitor in good standing in the alien capital. On several occasions, he was presented at court and had interviews with Duke Ching, to whom he administered some palatable doses of pungent criticism, so adroitly worded that they admitted of equivocal interpretations. In fact, the sugar-coating was so sweet that the unsuspecting duke swallowed the pills without being conscious of its bitter contents; he was delighted, but not helped.

A typical ruler of his time, Duke Ching, though old, indulged himself in the pleasures of the harem and the stable to the neglect of his state and people. Like many of his fellow aristocrats, senile and feeble-minded, he contemplated on deposing the legitimate heir in favor of a concubine's brat, thus setting loose a hell of squabbles among his sons. He also fell an easy victim to the fawning ministers, who knew how to prey on him by taking advantage of his mulishness. He was, what one might call, a father who was not a father, and a prince who was not a prince. The master of a thousand teams of horses in his lifetime, he was after death destitute of a single virtue with which to commemorate his name.

It was in answer to this ruler's question about government that Master K'ung spoke the following eight sphinx-like words that have since become classic: "Prince prince; minister minister; father father; son son." To put these terse, enigmatic substantives in their proper syntax so as to be more understandable, we would say: "Let the prince be a prince; the minister a minister; the father a father; and the son a son." The implication of this statement, as we see it today in the light of our knowledge of the duke's personality, is obvious enough; but the thick-witted aristocrat, misunderstanding its meaning, happily assented: "How true! For indeed when the prince is not a prince, the minister not a minister, the father not a father, the son not a son, though I have here my dish of millet, how can I live to enjoy it?"

On another day, while engaged with the duke in a conversation on the same subject, Master K'ung remarked: "Government consists in being sparing with the resources." It was sound advice, advocating economy, and the prince of a thousand teams of horses was vastly pleased with it, blind to the veiled satire and the irony that was so glaring.

5. *A Scathing Attack on the Man of* Li

These audiences turned out in K'ung Ch'iu's favor. The duke took a fancy to the visiting scholar from Lu, thinking that he had found in him the right man to run his government economically, so that he could have more horses in his stable. Here also was someone who could be trusted with upholding the feudal and paternal authority, of which he, the duke, was the personification in his state, but which, under the circumstances, was a bit shaky. So he made K'ung Ch'iu several attractive offers to induce him to stay at court. To be sure, the duke could not give the alien schoolman emoluments befitting a great minister of Ch'i, but he was willing to grant him a revenue between what the Chi and the Meng heads were getting for their services in Lu. Consequently he offered Master K'ung a fief at Lin-ch'iu, but the Master, more interested in guiding the prince to good government than in gilding his own interests, declined. It was against his principle to receive rewards that were not won by merit.

Thus on account of his moral scruples, K'ung Ch'iu lost his first and only chance of advancement in Ch'i. It never came to him again. The duke was still favorably disposed towards him, and on another occasion wished to enfeoff him with the fields of Ni-chi. But by this time, the courtiers of Ch'i, alarmed at the sudden turn of their ruler's favor towards this foreign scholar who was so unlike them, united in their efforts to disparage him before the duke. Even Yen Ying, a worthy minister of Ch'i, with whom K'ung Ch'iu was on friendly terms, felt the sting of jealousy and joined them in a scathing attack on K'ung Ch'iu as the "man of *li*":

These scholars (*ju*), being sophisticated and uncanny, cannot be taken as a norm; arrogant and self-conceited, they make bad subjects. They exalt funeral ceremonies and give vent to their mourning grief; they waste their substance on expensive burials and cannot be relied on to set an example for the people's manners. Travelling about to enrich themselves at the expense of the rulers, they cannot be entrusted with the government of the states. Since the great sages have passed away and the house of Chou has degenerated, rites and music become defective and incomplete. Now this Master K'ung has a thousand peculiarities. He flourishes in appearances and ornaments, complicates the ceremonials of reception and departure, elaborates on the customs of walking and bowing, so that many generations would not be enough to exhaust his teaching, and entire years not sufficient to plumb his rules of propriety (*li*). If your lordship wishes to employ him to change the manners of the country, you are not making the common people your primary concern.[7]

This was a death-blow to Master K'ung's prospects in Ch'i. The combined opposition of the ministers overrode their lord's fickle decision; slanders oft repeated had a semblance of truth. At last the duke was convinced that he had no longer any use for the Lu pedagogue. In disposing of his services, he gave a lame excuse: "I am too old to employ him."

Thus baffled in the unpredictable game of politics in a strange country bristling with hostility,[8] disillusioned though unbroken in spirit, Master K'ung retraced his steps back to Lu. (circa 515 B.C.)[9] Here after an absence of almost two years, he found that conditions had not improved much. The coun-

7. Though I quote here this speech by Yen Ying as reported by Ssu-ma Ch'ien, I rather doubt its authenticity.

8. According to one story, Master K'ung was in danger of being assassinated in Ch'i by his political adversaries.

9. There is some controversy about the date of Master K'ung's return to Lu. One theory advanced by the orthodox school is that Master K'ung could not possibly go back to his native state while the duke was still in exile. Consequently, the date of Master K'ung's return was postponed until 510 B.C., the year of Duke Chao's death. This made the Master's stay in Ch'i a total of seven years. But, in the mean time, Master K'ung was also supposed to have attended a funeral for the son of a Wu (an eastern state) envoy somewhere near the border of Lu in 515 B.C. To solve this dilemma, the critics asserted that the Master returned to Lu in that year specially for the funeral and then went back to Ch'i again. This seems to be much far-fetched. The easiest way is to make Master K'ung return to Lu in 515 B.C., as suggested here. (See Ch'ien Mu, *An Interlinking Chronology*, pp. 9–10.)

try was still seething with disorder, while the dispossessed duke lingered on the outskirts of his homeland without being able to re-enter. What indeed could a humble, though ambitious, scholar like K'ung Ch'iu do, if anything, to set to rights this unfortunate state of affairs? There was only one path open to him. Once more he settled down to teaching and study, perhaps in preparation for some better days when he would be called upon to take up a more responsible position than to reign over a schoolroom of wide-eyed youngsters.

Notwithstanding all these disappointments, Master K'ung had not made his trip to Ch'i in vain. If he had failed politically to gain a foothold there, he certainly had had ample recompense in the aesthetic pleasures which he experienced. For the first time in his ardent ritualistic life he was initiated into the beauties of *Shao,* a symbolic form of dance music supposed to have been composed by Shun (2255?–2204? B.C.), a sage emperor of pre-historic times. Even in Lu and the royal domain at Lo, the two great centers of ancient culture, Master K'ung had failed to hear the *Shao* music; here in Ch'i he heard it for the first time. As the story goes, he was so engrossed in its exalting melodies that for three months he was oblivious to the taste of meat. "I never imagined," he asserted, "that any music could be as excellent as this!"

6. *A Digression into Master K'ung's Private Life*

For the next fourteen years from 515 to 501 B.C., Master K'ung led a peaceful life in Lu as a private citizen. He was glad to have a chance, after those tempestuous days in Ch'i, to retire to the happy seclusion of his sanctuary of learning, where he had a continually expanding circle of zealous adherents. His fame as a scholar was such that recruits came flocking to him not only from Lu, but from all over the Chinese world, including the remote states of Ch'in and Ch'u. The majority of them gathered and dispersed as the years went by, but there also assembled around the Master a small band of the elect, who basked in the genial warmth of his affection, and who found a continuous source of inspiration in their daily contact with him, in "the feast of reason and the flow of soul," which they all enjoyed together. Inexhaustible was his fount of wisdom, for he was ever nourishing himself with new knowledge while he was imparting it.

As we have stated above, Master K'ung started his career as a teacher of ceremonies and music. These subjects he continued to pursue with an increasing zeal and insight until he himself became the epitome of what he had taught. He was very fond of vocal and instrumental music. Whenever he was in the company of one who sang well, he would make him repeat the song, while he himself accompanied it with his own voice. His favorite instruments were *ch'ing*, a music stone, and *ch'in*, a zither, also known as the scholar's lute. Indeed, he was such a fervent believer in music and its transforming effects that his enthusiasm caught fire among his disciples. One of his students, who later became the commandant of a walled town in Lu, took it upon himself to instruct his people in music as the first principle of government. Later, when the Master visited the place and heard the spirited sound of singing and stringed instruments, he was so delighted that he fell into a jocular mood. "Why use an ox-cleaver to kill a fowl?" laughed he roguishly. Upon his student-governor's protest at this irrelevant witticism, he apologized: "What I said just now was only in sport."

Though Master K'ung had a keen sense of humor, he was always observant of the proprieties; and as fond as he was of singing, he would desist from it on the day he had been wailing at a funeral. Neither would he eat his fill when seated by the side of a mourner. Whenever he walked past someone clad in the garb of sorrow, he would quicken his steps, or, if he was driving, bow to him over the cross-bar of his carriage. If a friend died without kith and kin to bury his remains, he would make it his care to administer the last rites to the deceased, saying, "The funeral is my affair."

In his daily life, Master K'ung was scrupulous in the observance of feudal customs and gentlemanly etiquette. Take, for instance, his eating habits. He would not sit down to his meals unless the mat was properly placed. He did not eat much and in the course of a sumptuous meal, would rise to his feet with a changed countenance to show his disapproval of over-indulgence. But when he was preparing himself for a sacrifice, he did not object to the rice's being of the finest quality, nor to the meat's being well minced. Moldy rice, putrid fish, and tainted meat he would not touch; nor would he dip his chopsticks in anything that was discolored, smelly, badly cooked, or out-of-season. Nor would he eat dishes which were prepared with the wrong sauce, or in which the meat was not properly cut. On the other hand, he preferred to have a balanced diet of vegetables and meat, well seasoned with a sprinkling of ginger, so that his breath would not smell of pork. To wine alone he set no limit, but he refused to drink any that was not home-brewed. Though most certainly no teetotaler, nor was he a habitual toper. As a matter of principle, he was careful not to get himself befuddled with excessive drinking.

In matters of clothing he was even more particular. It seems that by this time Master K'ung was well-to-do enough to have a large wardrobe of fur robes and other fine apparel. Though by no means a dandy, he was nevertheless a well-dressed gentleman, aesthetically fastidious about the colors and measurements of his dresses. He was never arrayed in maroon or scarlet; nor would he wear pink or roan for everyday. With a black robe he wore black lambskin; with a robe of undyed silk, fawn; and with a yellow robe, fox fur. When he went on visits of condolence, he was careful not to wear dark mouton lamb or hats of black-dyed silk, the Chinese mourning-color being white. For winter wear at home he used the thicker furs of the fox or badger, sometimes a long fur-cuffed robe with the right sleeve shorter than the left, so as to give his hand plenty of freedom. On hot summer days, far from being a nudist, he wore an unlined gown of loosely woven fine thread, and over it, when he went out, an outer garment.

Later, when Master K'ung took up official positions in Lu, his meticulous observance of court manners and proprieties continued to be highly exemplary, though to us moderns, unaccustomed to the pomposity of oriental monarchs, ridiculously eccentric. A true man of *li*, he gave to his prince what was due him, namely, homage and obeisance. Though accused by his enemies of fawning and cringing, Master K'ung stuck to his ceremonial practices, from which he never deviated. To begin with he would strut to the court in his splendid ceremonial robe, the many pieces of polished jade suspended from his girdle, jingling in merry melody as he walked. Then, stooping and bending, he would contract himself further, as he entered the palace gate, as though there were not enough room for him. He would not halt in the middle of the gateway, and while going through it, would decorously take care not to tread upon the threshold. When he approached the princely seat, a look of awful confusion would spread over his face, his groggy legs would wobble under him, and words would fail him. Then, lifting the hem of his robe, he would mount briskly to the audience hall, bow in obeisance, and hold his breath as if he were not breathing at all. Whether summoned to the presence of the duke, or acting as a ceremonial assistant in the reception of honored guests, or holding the jade tablet symbolic of the ruler's investiture, he always behaved in the staid, reverent, and decorous manner befitting the solemn occasion. At last, when the audience was over, his expression would suddenly relax into one of satisfaction and relief. He would quicken his pace as he reached the foot of the hall, and glide along with arms spread and the skirt of his robe fluttering as if in flight.

To watch Master K'ung eating and dressing, sacrificing and attending court, would be an unforgettable experience. Unfortunately, no such drawing has been handed down to posterity.[10] Early descriptions of him are so fabulously absurd,— he was represented as a fellow nine feet, six inches tall, with the form of a dragon, the lips of a buffalo, the palms of a tiger, the spine of a tortoise, and the mouth of an ocean,—that they make him more of a monster than a human being. As for his portraits, the earliest copy extant, the genuineness of which is very much in doubt, came down from the T'ang dynasty some thousand years or more after the Master's time. Practically all these likenesses were the children of the artists' roving imagination, with a good deal of make-up and inadvertent anachronism. He was, for instance, depicted as wearing the costumes of a much later period and in a setting entirely alien to the Chou era. Sometimes we see Master K'ung in his early twenties with beard and whiskers, looking sagaciously dignified and awe-inspiring, but no longer lusty and young.

Little is known about the domestic life of Master K'ung. There is no record whatsoever of the part his wife played, if any, in his distinguished career. Probably he and his wife did not get along well, and judging from his ritualistic idiosyncrasies, we would venture to say that it would have been hard for any woman to share a life of companionship with him. Rumor has it that he divorced his good spouse, as did his father before him and his grandson after him. If that were true, it would seem that such a practice must have persisted among the progenitors of the K'ung clan, none of whom, to be sure, was a lady's man. Besides his son Li, who was in constant

10. For a discussion of Master K'ung's portraits, see Berthold Laufer, "Confucius and his Portraits" in *The Open Court*, Chicago, 1912, XXVI, 147–68; 202–18.

attendance on him as a pupil, Master K'ung had a daughter married to one of his students; to another he gave to wife his niece, the daughter of his crippled brother Po-ni. But for these isolated incidents, Master K'ung's private life is shrouded in the heavy mantle of oblivious time. It was as a public figure, and not as a private individual, that he shone in the intellectual and official circles of Lu.

CHAPTER FIVE

The Official Life
of Master K'ung

1. *Master K'ung Receives the Gift of a Pig*

AT THE VIGOROUS AGE OF FORTY (511 B.C.) MASTER K'UNG NO longer suffered from perplexities. He had no misgivings now as to the correctness of his conduct or his mode of living; he was no longer perturbed by the scruples of his mind or the unsettled conditions of the state. It took him ten years more, however, when he reached fifty (501 B.C.), to understand what the biddings of Heaven were. After that he spoke openly of the mission of his life with true conviction.

The practical means of earning a living he looked down upon. When asked about gardening and farming, he disdainfully dismissed the subject by referring the inquirer to the old farmers and gardeners. On another occasion, a villager criticized him for having accomplished nothing to bear out his great reputation. Hearing this, he remarked peevishly to his followers: "What shall I do? Shall I take up chariot-driving? Or will it be archery? I think I'd better take up driving!"

On the other hand, teaching was still nearest to his heart, and he made use of those long, quiet years to perfect himself in the six arts, and, in addition, the art of poetry, with which to give vent to his sentiments and aspirations. He used to say in those days that a man's life should be exalted by poetry, strengthened by rituals, and consummated through music. About the same time, he plunged into the study of history, the official documents of antiquity and the annals of the feudal states. Divination began to allure him with its rich, mythical lore, but he was not yet ready for it, and several years elapsed before he found his mind attuned to these metaphysical disquisitions on the dark mysteries of life.

This was then the most formative period of Master K'ung's intense intellectual life. But if he had fallen in love with the fair Muses, there were other moments in which he was attracted to the charm of politics, from which he could not completely wean himself since these hectic Ch'i days. Was not his hero, the Duke of Chou, the greatest political genius that had ever lived? Did not the Duke's achievements culminate in the government reforms he had brought about, and the feudal institutions he had established? Was it not because of him that the Chinese world was able to enjoy a long, flourishing period of peace and prosperity unrivaled in its history? The great Duke had made a practical application of his moral principles and intellectual knowledge to the benefit of his state and people. Why couldn't he, K'ung Ch'iu, aspire to the same? These then must have been the recurring undercurrents of thought that surged and ebbed in the busy brain of our Heaven-commissioned schoolman as he was fast approaching his fiftieth year.

But there was one great barrier to his political aspirations. He could not see his way clear to taking up public duties in Lu so long as the path of officialdom was beset with thorns. To be sure, after the death of the exiled Chao in 510 B.C., a new ruler, Duke Ting (B.C. 509–495), had been placed on the ducal seat, but he remained, as did his predecessors, a puppet in the hands of the three powerful clans. And what was worse, even the great ministers themselves were now being tyrannized by their subordinates, their own family stewards. It was not a vicious cycle, but an interlocking chain of usurpation, with the Chou sovereign bullied by his vassals, the feudal lords by their ministers, and the noble officers, in their turn, by their retainers. These last were usually wardens of some walled towns that belonged to the baronial families. Backed up by the armed strength of the townsfolk, who owed fealty to their immediate superiors rather than to their absentee lords, they were the de facto commandants of these outlying fortresses. Some of the more aggressive and seditious fellows stayed in the capital to take part in court intrigues and to arrogate for themselves the governmental power that their own masters had seized in the same unscrupulous manner from the reigning prince.

The worst example of such official insubordination was to be found in Lu, where among the retainers of the Chi household there rose Yang Hu, the most villainous political upstart known in these feudal times. It happened that by 505 B.C., the year of Chi P'ing-tzu's death, the three noble clans were all headed by inexperienced young scions, who could not command respect among their unruly followers. Sensing the situation, Yang Hu, as the chief steward of the most powerful baronial house, took this opportunity to seize the Lu government. He first purged the Chi household of his rivals and enemies, and then to anticipate the protest of his young master Huan-tzu, took him prisoner and exacted from him a sworn covenant. The next year he sent Meng I-tzu (Ho-chi), who had been K'ung Ch'iu's pupil, on a diplomatic mission to Tsin, while at home he imposed another altar-oath not only upon the three noble clans, but upon the duke and the people of Lu as well, with the imprecations publicly declaimed at the Road of the Five Fathers in the capital. Later (503 B.C.), he led the ministers Meng and Chi in an expedition against the invading Ch'i soldiers and by his stupidity almost plunged

the Lu army into a disastrous defeat. After the evacuation of
the enemy forces from Yang-kuan, a Lu city, he converted it
into a stronghold of his own.

Yang Hu was now virtually dictator of the Lu state. To
consolidate and expand further his power in the government
he was anxious to enlist in his camp men of talent and renown.
And none other, it seemed to him, was more desirable than
K'ung Ch'iu, the famous schoolman, whose growing popularity and influence, through his many pupils, was beginning to
be felt in the capital. But the Master appeared to hold himself
aloof from all political contacts, and especially from the insinuating advances of Yang Hu. Realizing Master K'ung's indifference, Yang Hu tried to ensnare the high-brow who had
so persistently avoided an interview with him. So he watched
closely for Master K'ung's whereabouts, and one day when the
latter was away from home, he sent to his house the present of a
suckling pig. When Master K'ung returned and saw the pig
from the usurping minister, he knew at once that he had been
caught in a trap. How could he help going and bowing at
Yang Hu's door in acknowledgment of the gift he was not
able to receive personally, such being the etiquette on the occasion of a present from a high official to a member of the
humble *shih* class, to which Master K'ung belonged?

Master K'ung however was undaunted. He knew how to
meet guile with guile. Watching for a time when Yang Hu was
not at home, he went there to pay his respects for the gift. It
was a very clever maneuver successfully executed by the good
pedagogue. But unfortunately for him, while he was on his
way home from the ceremonial visit, lo! whom should he meet
face to face but the infamous Yang Hu himself!

"Come, let me speak with you," beckoned the elated scholar-
baiter. "Can one who cherishes his jewel in his bosom and lets
his country go to the dogs be called good?"

"Certainly not."

"Can one who longs to take part in public affairs, yet time after time loses the opportunity to do so—can such a one be called wise?"

"Certainly not."

"The days and months are gliding by; the years do not tarry for us!"

"All right," growled Master K'ung in exasperation, "I'll go into office!"

2. *The Scholar-Magistrate of Chung-Tu*

We have no idea how Master K'ung finally extricated himself from this desperate promise he made to Yang Hu against his better judgment. It was not that he was reluctant to take official positions. On the contrary, he was yearning for a chance to make use of his immense knowledge of history and government, rituals and ethics, in the administration of the state and the uplifting of his fellow men. But herein was the rub. The man who offered to employ him was an unprincipled upstart who had tyrannized over the people and officials of Lu, and who was exactly the kind of man Master K'ung would like to dispose of, if he had his way in the government. Potential office-seeker though he was, he would under no circumstances sneak into officialdom by the backdoor to work for such a scoundrel as Yang Hu.

Delay was probably the best and the safest tactic in Master K'ung's case. And he had not long to wait, for soon afterwards Yang Hu got so puffed up that he courted his own downfall by an unsuccessful coup d'état to assassinate his master Huan-tzu in 502 B.C. He was defeated by the loyal followers of the three noble clans, and fled to the border town of Yang-kuan, where he held out for yet another year before he was finally driven out of the state.

In the meantime, Master K'ung had another invitation to office from the warden of Pi, the chief citadel of the Chi family.

Kung-shan Fu-jao, a steward of the Chi, was a confederate of Yang Hu, and like the latter had seditious ambitions against his master. But he was not as notorious as Yang Hu, and since his ultimate intention was unknown, Master K'ung hoped that he might influence the Pi governor for the good of the state by making him instrumental in restoring the reigning duke to his rightful powers. So he was inclined to go to Pi, but desisted upon his student Tzu-lu's remonstrance. It is almost pathetic to listen to the frustrated idealist lamely justifying his motive for accepting the invitation: "It cannot be for nothing that he (Kung-shan Fu-jao) has sent for me. If I could be used, I could still make an Eastern Chou."

If Master K'ung had been dreaming fondly of establishing in Lu, or any other principality in the East, a new seat of feudal greatness, comparable to the prosperous Western kingdom originally set up by the Duke of Chou, an opportunity, at least, for its realization did present itself at long last. In 501 B.C., the ninth year of Duke Ting, his great official career in Lu began. Mellowed by experience and learning, wise in his knowledge of the hoary past, and strong in his personal integrity and humaneness, K'ung Ch'iu created a tremendous sensation among the official circles of Lu by his phenomenal success in government administration and diplomatic dealings. For a time, it seems, he almost succeeded in raising an Eastern Chou out of the debris of the fast crumbling dynasty; and probably would have achieved his purpose had not hostile forces, increasing in power as they gathered from all quarters, combined to wreck this infant Utopia of Master K'ung's creation.

At the age of fifty, Master K'ung was a prominent figure in Lu. The repeated invitations to office from Yang Hu and Kung-shan Fu-jao, both of which he had turned down, showed his popularity even among the group of unruly officials. But now with Yang Hu happily out of the way, the path was clear for Master K'ung's rise to greatness. Since the three hereditary ministers from the aristocratic families were still novices in state affairs, the authority of the reigning duke was not completely overshadowed. Moreover, I-tzu, the Meng chief, had once been a ceremonial apprentice in the schoolroom of K'ung, and though he was now a great minister of state, their pupil-teacher relationship continued. All these added to the Master's prestige and assured his chance of promotion.

Master K'ung first took office as the chief magistrate of Chung-tu, an outlying town some twenty-eight miles west of the capital. Immediately upon taking office, he undertook a great reformation in the manners and morals of the people. A ritual zealot, he eagerly introduced to the government of the town the feudal ideals of the good old days of Chou, enacting laws for the nourishment of the living as well as the burial of the dead. Different foods were prescribed for the young and old, and tasks commensurate with their strength and weakness. In funeral observances, he regulated the proper thickness of the inner and outer coffins in accordance with ancient standards; he also initiated the custom of burial on the hillsides, thereby sparing the people the trouble of raising artificial mounds over the graves, a contemporary practice which, it will be recalled, Master K'ung himself had followed to his chagrin when he interred his parents together at Fang. But his crowning achievement was in the province of morals. He pursued his policy of sex segregation so vigorously that men and women walked on opposite sides of the street, and he hammered at honesty so assiduously that objects lost on the street were not picked up.

The fame of Master K'ung's success spread far and wide. The duke was vastly impressed and asked him whether the same principles could be adapted to governing the state. "Oh, certainly they could," replied the ambitious magistrate of Chung-tu, "not only in the government of Lu, but the whole world as well!"

It is a moot question whether Master K'ung advanced directly from the wardenship of Chung-tu to the Ministry of Crime, or whether he had been made the Minister of Works during the interval. The latter position was hereditary in the Meng family, and if Master K'ung ever took office there, he must have served either in the capacity of an assistant or a deputy to the minister, who was none other than his student I-tzu. It is quite possible that for some reasons unknown to us, probably on account of sickness or absence, I-tzu had entrusted the administration of his department temporarily to his renowned teacher. But his period of incumbency was short, if it ever existed, for before long Master K'ung was given the important post of the Minister of Crime, next in rank only to the ministries of Instruction, Works, and War held by the heads of the three aristocratic families.

It was about this time that Master K'ung exercised his authority to remedy the wrongs done by the Chi clan to Chao, the deceased duke. When the exiled prince had died at Kan-hou in 510 B.C., his coffin had been brought back to Lu for interment in the family burial grounds. But instead of depositing him side by side with his forebears, Chi P'ing-tzu, pursuing his hatred of the unfortunate duke even to his grave, had placed Chao's tomb apart from the others on the south of the road leading to the ducal cemetery. This was, according to the feudal standards of the period, an outrageous act, which K'ung Ch'iu took upon himself to right. He could not very well remove the grave from where it had already stood for almost ten years, but by a clever stroke of genius, he hit upon the wonderful expediency of surrounding the entire graveyard with a ditch, thus connecting the lonely tomb of Chao with the main ducal group. Then, addressing Huan-tzu, the Chi head, Master K'ung said: "To humiliate the prince by m⌐king a display of his guilt is contrary to propriety. I have united the tombs so as to hide your father's disloyalty."

3. *The New Minister of Crime*

In 500 B.C., Master K'ung was promoted to the Ministry of Crime, the highest non-hereditary office that any citizen of Lu could aspire to hold. His remarkable success in reforming the morals of his fellow men during his magistracy of Chung-tu particularly fitted him for the task of administering justice to the people. In the place of severe laws and cruel punishments, —and in those days penalties could be barbarously cruel,[1]—he introduced moral education as the most effective means of combating crime. When everyone became upright and honest, he contended, there would be little cause for wickedness and depravity. "In hearing litigations," said the new Minister of Crime, "I am like everybody else. The best thing to do is to make litigations unnecessary."

It is no fallacy to say that the appointment of Master K'ung as the Minister of Crime put an end to all crimes. Through the centuries, Chinese scholars have been fond of enumerating, and sometimes inventing, stories of the Master's achievements as the supreme justice of state. According to one account, there were in Lu a butcher who cheated his customers by blowing water into his sheep every morning he went to market; an old dotard who dared not put a rein to his wife's lechery; and a rich bully who indulged in the luxury of violating the statutes. But so fearful were they of the new minister's punitive measures that by the time Master K'ung was installed in his office, the tradesman had stopped his dishonest practice, the patriarch had divorced his dissolute spouse, and the wealthy lawbreaker had fled the state.

Another anecdote relates to Master K'ung's sympathy for

1. The common corporal punishments were castration, the cutting off of feet, hands, or knee-cap, branding, and flogging. Death penalties included hanging, decapitation, and the more barbarous practices of quartering, boiling the culprit alive, and having him torn to pieces by chariots pulled by horses in opposite directions.

the underdog. In a lawsuit between a father and his son, the supreme justice threw them both into prison, showing no partiality in his treatment of the two litigants. Then after three months, at the father's request, he released them. Huantzu, head of the Chi family, not being able to justify this, complained that the Minister of Crime was trifling with him. "Formerly he used to tell me that filial piety comes first in the government of the state. Such being the case, why didn't he put this unfilial son to death as an example to all the people?"

Hearing this criticism, Master K'ung heaved a deep sigh and said: "Alas! it is not right for superiors to fail in their duty and then insist on having their inferiors put to death! To punish those untutored in filial devotion is to slay the guiltless. No soldiers should be punished for the defeat of the three armies. If the prison laws are not in order, no offender should be penalized for his ignorance. Why? Because the superiors have not carried out their instructions, and hence the fault does not lie in the common people."

It was also in the heyday of Master K'ung's great power, when he became, according to one account, the acting prime minister,[2] that he executed from among the dignitaries of Lu a political agitator, Shao-cheng Mao by name. For this rigorous action, the Master was gently upbraided by his pupils, but he defended himself vigorously by accusing Shao-cheng Mao of being a dangerous demagogue, whose subversive activities con-

2. Whether Master K'ung had ever acted as prime minister is a question much debated upon by Chinese scholars. In the latter days of the Warring States period, the story of Master K'ung's having been acting premier already gained currency. This was confirmed by Hsing Ch'ing, the greatest K'ung scholar of the time, and followed by Ssu-ma Ch'ien in his "Life of K'ung-tzu." But some of the more critical scholars doubted the possibility of the Master's ever assuming such a high office, which was hereditary with the heads of the Chi family. They contended that the Chinese word for premier might also mean "ritual assistant," a post which Master K'ung actually held when he accompanied the duke of Lu on a diplomatic conference to Ch'i. Among Western scholars, Legge took this latter view. (See Legge, *Chinese Classics*, I, "Prolegomena," p. 74.)

stituted a threat to the peace of the state. Even in the face of the bitterest criticism, if he believed he was in the right, K'ung Ch'iu, the honest magistrate, would not flinch from using his authority to rid the country of its pests. And had he not the illustrious example of the Duke of Chou who killed his own brothers Kuan and Ts'ai because of their revolt against the Son of Heaven?[3]

4. *A Ceremonial Triumph in a Treacherous Diplomatic Conference*

All these accomplishments were credit enough to Master K'ung, but the most sensational success that crowned his official career was a diplomatic triumph he scored at a meeting of the princes of Lu and Ch'i at Chia-ku in the summer of 500 B.C., shortly after he became the Minister of Crime. As will be remembered, the long peace between Lu and the other Chinese states was broken in 503 B.C., when the armies of Ch'i invaded the western borders of Lu. But now with the banishment of Yang Hu, and K'ung Ch'iu's subsequent rise to power, Lu once more enjoyed a period of unmatched prosperity, while its position abroad was also greatly strengthened. In consequence, a meeting of the two rulers was agreed upon as a highly desirable means of settling old scores and possibly of forming a new tie of friendship between the two neighboring states. Here in Lu, amidst the many preparations going on for this great event, K'ung Ch'iu, the man of *li*, was appointed, as was but natural, the master of ceremonies to accompany the ducal party to Ch'i. Even in these degenerate days, success in

3. Of King Wen's many sons, Fa (King Wu) was the second; Hsien (Kuan-shu), the third; Tan (Duke of Chou), the fourth; Tu (Ts'ai-shu), the fifth, etc. After the death of King Wu, his young son Cheng came to the throne with the Duke of Chou as regent. Inflamed by jealousy and suspicion, Kuan-shu and Ts'ai-shu, who had been previously enfeoffed respectively at Kuan and Ts'ai, turned against King Cheng in alliance with the Shang people. The revolt, however, was quelled by the Duke of Chou. Kuan-shu was killed, and Ts'ai-shu, either banished or killed.

an interstate conference depended not so much upon verbal victories as upon the proper observance of elaborate rituals, which no ruler could afford to ignore on such solemn occasions.

When the news of Master K'ung's appointment reached Ch'i, its ministers had a good laugh up their sleeves. What had a pedantic visionary to do with present-day politics? What did he know about diplomatic intrigues and double-dealings? So they happily conspired to lay a booby trap for the Lu visitors at the coming conference, with the hope that, when caught in the snare and threatened with death, the prince of Lu would be more than willing to yield to the terms demanded of him.

Master K'ung, however, was not a mere ritualist, a dry-as-dust pedagogue incapable of quick decisions and prompt actions. On the contrary, he was equal to every occasion. When circumstances demanded it, he could be shrewd and resourceful as a seasoned politician, daring and resolute as a veteran warrior. Moreover, he possessed a rare insight into human nature, and an even rarer intuition of the possible shape of things to come, and of the storm that was now brewing. He knew but too well the kind of man his old friend was,—that capricious Duke Ching of Ch'i,—with his coterie of parasitic courtiers who fed and fattened themselves on his gullibility. And wasn't Master K'ung thoroughly conversant with their unscrupulous dealings in the early days when he himself was a victim of their treachery? Though many years had passed, he was sure that as long as the erratic Ching was still holding the reins of government, the calibre of his ministers could not be very much improved. One thing at least was certain—the Ch'i officials were *not* to be trusted.

Duke Ting was ready to set out on his journey to Ch'i in a single chariot, as if on a friendly visit. But Master K'ung, who knew better, cautioned him: "I have heard that one should make martial preparations when attending a civil conference, just as one should make peaceful preparations in a military consultation. In ancient times, the feudal lords always took along their entire official retinue whenever they left the boundaries of their principality. I beg your lordship to take with you the Right and Left Ministers of War." Consequently the duke went to the meeting with a military escort.

At Chia-ku in the territory of Ch'i, there was built for the occasion a terraced platform with a three-tiered earthen stairway leading to it. After much bowing and yielding to precedence in conformity with feudal etiquette, the two princes of Ch'i and Lu mounted the steps together. After the rites had been consummated by a pledge of friendship with a ceremonial cup of wine, an official of Ch'i addressed Duke Ching thus: "I beg that the Music of the Four Quarters be played." Thereupon, a band of aborigines, decked in pheasant feathers and ox-tails, and holding spears and lances, swords and shields, rushed to the scene amidst a furious medley of drums and warcries.

This was the moment that Master K'ung was expecting. But he was undaunted, for he was well girded for the emergency. Hastening forward and up the staircase, he stood still next to the last step; and raising his broad sleeves, he said: "Our two princes are gathered for a friendly conference. What business has the music of the barbarians here? I request that instructions be given to the attending officers to dismiss them."[4] But

4. I follow Ssu-ma Ch'ien in this intense and vivid narrative, though perhaps a little exaggerated for dramatic effect. The *Tso's Commentary*, generally accepted as more historical, reported rather pedantically of Master K'ung's speech as follows: "Let the soldiers smite them (the dancers)! Our two princes are met here on terms of friendship, and for those captives from the barbarous tribes to throw the gathering into confusion with their weapons is not the way for the prince of Ch'i to command the feudal lords. Those aboriginal people have nothing to do with us Chinese; those wild tribes must not be permitted to create disorder on our flowery lands; prisoners of war should not break in upon a covenant; weapons should not threaten a friendly meeting. As before the spirits, such a thing is inauspicious; in point of virtue, it is contrary to what is right; and between man and man, it is a failure in propriety. Your lordship must not act thus." (Legge, *Chinese Classics*, V, 777.)

the uncouth dancers refused to go, and the entire company turned their eyes towards the noble host. Ashamed, the duke of Ch'i ordered the unwelcome entertainers to be removed.

A few moments later, an official of Ch'i came forward to say: "I beg that the Music of the Inner Palace be performed." Duke Ching nodded, and soon after clowns and dwarfs appeared. As before, Master K'ung again remonstrated, saying: "Such scurvy fellows who dare to corrupt our princes deserve death. I request that orders for their execution be given to the officers-in-charge." As the entertainers were being executed, "their hands and feet flew apart."

After these ceremonial rebuffs, the Ch'i prince made one more attempt to entrap his noble compeer. He invited Duke Ting as an honored guest to a state dinner. But Master K'ung declined for his lord on proper ritualistic grounds, saying that with business over, to make preparations for a regal feast would only entail additional labor and trouble to the attending officials; and, furthermore, that "banquet is for the purpose of displaying virtue; if virtue is not exalted, it is better to have no entertainment."

Neither could Ch'i overreach its rival state in the wording of their pact. The treaty, as first read on the part of Ch'i, ran: "So be it to Lu, the curse of this covenant, if you do not follow us with three hundred chariots of war when the army of Ch'i crosses its border." But Master K'ung immediately retaliated by sending a messenger to add to it the Lu amendment: "And so be it to Ch'i, if without restoring to us the fields south of the river Wen, you expect us to obey your behests."

Disgraced and outmaneuvered by the "man of ceremonies," Duke Ching of Ch'i was so thoroughly ashamed of himself and his intriguing ministers that he straightway returned to Lu, in accordance with the terms of the covenant, all the territories he had taken from her by force.

5. The City Walls Are Razed

After this diplomatic triumph over Ch'i, Lu's position in the family of Chinese states became well established. Home again in the capital, Master K'ung fostered there the same moral reforms that he had brought about in Chung-tu. Once more, sex segregation, moral probity, and the proper observance of ceremonies were the order of the day. Strangers, who came to Lu from all sides, found themselves received with such hospitality that they felt as if they were returning to their own land.

It certainly seemed to Master K'ung that the state of Lu was on its way towards a golden age similar to that of Kings Wen and Wu. There was, however, one thing that worried him. The reigning duke was still not strong enough to assert his authority over the three clans, who had for generations arrogated his rightful powers. Could Master K'ung, now a strong man in Lu, do something to remove this one great stumbling-block to feudal restoration? He had found out that the strength of the three families lay in their walled cities, whose inhabitants, when armed for the wrong cause, could be a menace to the security of both the state and its prince. Something therefore should be done to clip the wings of their military might and thereby to reduce their insubordination at court.

"Yes, the fortified towns must be destroyed!" cried Master K'ung.

A favorable opportunity now presented itself for such fearless undertaking. In the course of time, these walled citadels proved as much a headache to the prince as to the heads of the noble families who held them in fief. Nominally they were lords of these baronial seats, but in fact they were absentee owners who resided most of the time in the capital far from their feudal holdings. Thus the allegiance of the people, whom they did not command personally, shifted to their family ministers, who had direct control of these towns. And seditious stewards like Yang Hu, more dangerous to their immediate masters than to the reigning duke, were not lacking among members of the three aristocratic households.

The conflict between the barons and their disloyal retainers seems to have reached its peak in this period of Lu history. The first serious outbreak occurred as early as 530 B.C. when a mutinous commander of Pi held the city against the Chi family for two years before he was finally subdued. Then there was the intractable Yang Hu, who, as we have seen, attempted the assassination of his lord Huan-tzu, seized the duke as a hostage in the insurrection, and, when defeated, robbed the ducal palace of its treasured heirlooms, a piece of precious jade and a great bow.[5] And now, immediately after the return of the ducal party from Chia-ku, the warden of Hou revolted against the Shu-sun family, and it was only after repeated sieges and through the clever ruse of a faithful officer, the superintendent engineer of the city, that the uprising was finally quelled. Meanwhile, Kung-shan Fu-jao, on whom Master K'ung once had placed such great hopes, was still solidly entrenched behind the ramparts of Pi, waiting for an opportune time to make Lu, not an ideal Eastern Chou, but a hotbed of political agitation.

The recent insurrection of the Hou warden gave Master K'ung a strong weapon with which to strike at the vulnerable position of the three barons, who found themselves trapped by the engines of their own influence. Taking advantage of this psychological moment, the Minister of Crime now made a bold move. He publicly proposed the dismantling of the baronial strongholds as an important step towards restoring the authority of the duke and securing peace for the state. He said to Duke Ting: "No subject should be allowed to keep armor

5. The bow was a highly treasured heirloom supposed to have been given to Po Ch'in, the first duke of Lu, by King Cheng in the 11th century B.C.

or weapons; no baron should possess a city with a hundred parapets."[6]

In his effort to centralize the ducal power, Master K'ung found a noble ally in his pupil Tzu-lu, who was then steward of the Chi family. In the duke's name, and with the happy connivance of the great ministers, the Master and pupil set themselves energetically to the formidable task of razing the fortified walls and outworks of the cities Pi, Hou, and Cheng that belonged respectively to the clans of Chi, Shu-sun, and Meng. The memory of its rebellion still fresh in his mind, Shu-sun first dismantled, in 498 B.C., the stronghold of Hou. The Chi family was about to follow suit, when Kung-shan Fu-jao marched to the capital at the head of his men in an open revolt. Taken by surprise, the duke and the ministers hastily retreated to the Chi palace to seek refuge in its fortified tower. But there they were attacked by the insurgents, some of whom had even penetrated the duke's forces. At this crucial moment, Master K'ung sent his own followers down to fight the swarming assailants. The men of Pi were put to rout; their walls were razed.

The Meng clan, however, held tenaciously to their city of Cheng. Its chief I-tzu, a former student of Master K'ung, pretended that he knew nothing about the whole affair and ignored the order for its dismantling. Thereupon, the duke, probably urged by the Minister of Crime, beleaguered Cheng in the twelfth month of the same year, but returned without being able to accomplish his mission.

Cheng would have offered no resistance, had Master K'ung had his way in Lu. But it seems that just at this very moment when he had reached the zenith of his great official career, heaped with honors and crowned with successes, the dark relentless forces of evil gathered to wreak their vengeance on

6. A parapet is about 30 feet; therefore, a wall of 100 parapets would be 3,000 feet long.

him. They dealt him such a crushing blow that he fell out of
the ring of politics altogether. But ironically enough, the
knockdown came not from the iron fist of an enemy, but the
soft, delicate hands of the dancing girls.

6. *Women and Horses*

To resolve the above riddle, we must return once more to
the conspiring ministers of Ch'i. After having suffered those
face-losing reverses in the Chia-ku conference, they were now
thoroughly alarmed at the rising comet of the man of *li,* whom
they could no longer lightly brush aside with a sneer. "If Master K'ung should remain in power, he would certainly obtain
hegemony for his state; and if he succeeds, Ch'i will be the first
to be annexed, because our land lies nearest to Lu." Thus
argued the officials of Ch'i in an emergency consultation. One
of them even proposed the cession of some Ch'i territory to
Master K'ung as a measure of appeasement. But at length, it
was agreed that before such a drastic step was taken, they
should first move heaven and hell, if necessary, to block K'ung
Ch'iu's power in Lu. It was then that they hit upon the idea of
trying on Duke Ting what is now known in Chinese phrase-
ology as the "stratagem of beauties." Thereupon they chose
eighty of the prettiest maidens of Ch'i, well trained in music
and the dance, and thirty teams of four horses each,—there is
no record whether these were taken from the spacious stables
of Duke Ching,—and sent them as a gesture of friendship to
the ruler of Lu.

The beautiful women and shiny steeds arrived outside the
south gate of the capital. They soon became the talk of the
town, and all flocked there to have a look. Among the crowd
was Huan-tzu, the great minister, who, to prevent criticism,
went incognito. Upon his persuasion, the duke too went to
take a look. Once there, he was so fascinated that the casual
drive turned out to be a whole day's affair. For three mornings

no audience was held. The wenches and horses were received into the palace, and the Sage was neglected.

Tzu-lu was indignant. He said to the Master: "Sir, it is time for us to quit." The Master replied: "The state is going to offer a sacrifice to Heaven. If the ministers are given the customary gift of sacrificial meat, I will yet choose to stay."

The ceremony was duly performed, but no sacrificial offerings were sent to the Minister of Crime. He had no alternative but to leave.

Accompanied by his small band of faithful followers, Master K'ung departed from Lu with a heavy heart, singing his song of sorrow, as he dragged his unwilling, lingering steps away from his native land:

> O the singing of these wenches
> Has driven me from here.
> O the coming of these wenches
> Brings death and ruin!
> O Woe! O Wandering!
> Even unto life's end![7]

7. Lin Yutang gives a free version of the song (*The Wisdom of Confucius*, p. 68) as follows:

> Beware of a woman's tongue,
> Sooner or later you'll get stung.
> Beware of a woman's visit,
> Sooner or later you'll get it.
> Heigh Ho! Heigh Ho!
> I'm going to run away.

CHAPTER SIX

Years of Wandering and Tribulation

•

1. *A Beautiful Jade for Sale*

"I HAVE HERE," SAID TZU-KUNG, ONE OF THE MASTER'S FAVORITE disciples, "a beautiful piece of jade. Should I hide it away in a casket, or should I seek for a good price to sell it?"

"Sell it, by all means!" was the Master's reply. "I too am waiting to be sold, at a right price."

*   *   *   *   *

The exact date and occasion of this piece of highly illuminating conversation is unknown. But it is apparent that at times Master K'ung seemed reluctant to enter office, and to draw him out on the subject, Tzu-kung made this clever, tactful inquiry about the jade, and got the Master's answer, which is candid to the extreme: he was waiting for a good offer, but the price had to be right.

This seems to be the keynote to all Master K'ung's activities during the fourteen years of his wanderings abroad (B.C. 497–484). It is disconcerting to reflect that in all these years, in which his steps covered the central states of Ts'ao, Wey, Sung, Cheng, Ch'en, Ts'ai, and even possibly Ch'u, he never met with a ruler good enough to listen to him seriously, or wise enough to entrust him with the government of his country. On the contrary, he was baffled and foiled, humiliated and threatened, without having a chance to make use of his rare talents and superior knowledge. The heavenly revelations of his fiftieth year were still vivid in his mind and continued to persist at sixty. "If any of the princes were to employ me," so he believed, "twelve months would be sufficient to achieve something. In the course of three years, all would be consummated." But Heaven denied him such favor, in spite of its manifest decree, and the many years of Master K'ung's travel were spent in tribulation,—an unfitting sequel to such a brilliant and promising career.

2. *Lust in Front, Virtue Behind*

It is next to impossible to reconstruct with satisfaction an exact chronology of Master K'ung's wandering life, and to note with accuracy the details of his visit to the various states. The years were many, but the records are scanty; and the few we have are so inconsistent and confusing that they present an ill-fitting and incomplete jig-saw puzzle. While it smacks of credulity to relate indiscriminately all the popular episodes about him, it is equally unwise to reject arbitrarily everything that rebels against the orthodox taste of a purist, or casts doubt in the catholic mind of an historian. The best we can do is to follow cautiously Ssu-ma Ch'ien's biography of the sage, ever bearing in mind that, though born 2000 years ago, the first historian had likewise great difficulty in weaving into a reliable account the loose threads of Master K'ung's life, undertaking the task, as he did, some 400 years after the sage's death.

Scholars all agree that the first state the Master visited was Wey, a small principality to the west of Lu, on the northern bank of the Yellow River. Here Master K'ung made his temporary home, and though he left it off and on as many as five times, according to Ssu-ma Ch'ien, it was also here that he lived the longest during these vagrant years. A little pedantic it may seem to delve into the causes of Master K'ung's making Wey the anchorage of his drifting bark, but it has been variously pointed out that many of his disciples came from Wey and that it was a populous state with great possibilities of development and growth. The Master certainly had a favorable impression of Wey as he rode through the country.

"How thriving is the population here!" he observed.

"Since it is so thriving," asked Jan Ch'iu, a disciple, who was driving the Master's chariot, "what more could one expect?"

"Enrich the people!"

"And when they are enriched?"

"Teach them!" was the Master's reply.

Thus with great hopes Master K'ung stopped in Wey, where he lodged at first in the home of Yen Ch'ou-yu, an honest official.[1] But there lived in Wey a Mi Hsia, Tzu-lu's brother-in-law and a favorite of Ling, the reigning duke. Talking to Tzu-lu one day, Mi Hsia said, "If Master K'ung would only accept my hospitality, he might be made a great minister of Wey." When Master K'ung heard of this, he remarked casually: "It will be as bidden."

Soon afterwards Master K'ung was presented to the prince, who offered him an annual emolument of 60,000 bushels of grain. There is no record of what office, if any, Master K'ung held in Wey. Probably it was just a sinecure to keep in the Wey court this renowned statesman from Lu, whose fame preceded him wherever he went. In fact Master K'ung must have been quite a curiosity in the Wey capital, and the duke's favorite wife, Nan-tzu, an attractive but dissolute woman, could not rest until she had had a look at the eminent visitor. Wishing a private audience with Master K'ung, therefore, she sent him the following message: "The gentlemen of the four quarters who do not disdain to form ties of fraternity with

1. In Ssu-ma Ch'ien's narrative, Yen Ch'ou-yu, with whom Master K'ung stayed, became Tzu-lu's brother-in-law. He had probably misread the account given by Meng K'o.

our lord are always presented to my insignificant self. She too desires to have the pleasure of your company." But though the lady was willing, the Sage was not. He politely declined the invitation. His refusal, however, did not avail him, for Nan-tzu was so insistent that Master K'ung was obliged, in spite of himself, to make the visit.

Let us picture the scene as the duchess, decked in her finery, sat behind a silken curtain, awaiting the scholarly visitor. Entering the inner apartment of her palace, K'ung Ch'iu saluted towards the north, as was the custom. Nan-tzu returned the salutation twice from behind the screen, and as she curtsied, her jade bracelets and pendants jingled and clanked merrily.

The Master, pleased with the presentation and ever conscious of the proprieties, told his students: "I really did not wish to visit her. Nevertheless, I have seen her, and she returned my greetings with decorum."

But Tzu-lu was displeased, whereupon Master K'ung took an oath, saying: "If I have done wrong, may Heaven forsake me, may Heaven forsake me!"

Master K'ung's sojourn in Wey was interrupted by a flitting visit to K'uang, a small dependency south of Wey. The reason for his sudden departure is not known, but one account has it that he felt himself shadowed by a secret service man in the duke's employ, though there is no clear explanation for such measure. Anyway, after having been there for ten months, Master K'ung left Wey for Ch'en, the goal of his journey. But as the Lu party was passing through K'uang, Yen Keh, the driver, pointing with his whip to a breach in the city wall, said excitedly within the hearing of the people, "This is where we broke into the city the last time." Now the devils were loosed, for the people, mistaking the Master for Yang Hu, who had once treacherously entered the city and oppressed its inhabitants, surrounded Master K'ung and detained him.

By this time Yen Hui, a favorite pupil, who had lagged behind, caught up with the party.

"I thought you had got killed," said Master K'ung.

"So long as the Master lives," replied the pupil, "how dare I die?"

All his followers were frightened at the incident, and so probably was the Master himself;[2] but he calmed them by saying: "Since the death of King Wen, is not the cause of Culture lodged here in me? If it be Heaven's will to destroy this Culture, posterity will never again share in its knowledge. But if Heaven will let it live, what can the men of K'uang do to me?"

As a show of composure, then, he ordered Tzu-lu to play on the zither, while he himself accompanied the song with his voice. Three times they sang the melody and, sure enough, the men of K'uang did no harm to Master K'ung. After they were satisfied with his true identity, they removed their "buff-coats," apologized, and withdrew.

His plan having been upset by this hapless adventure, Master K'ung retraced his steps to Wey. But because of another unfortunate incident, his stay there was also destined to be short. One day, about a month later, as Duke Ling was riding through the market-place in his grand ducal carriage, with the notorious Nan-tzu by his side, and Master K'ung following behind in a second vehicle, the crowds, gathered to witness the regal procession, suddenly burst forth with the cry: "Lust in the front, virtue behind!"

Thoroughly ashamed of himself for having got into such a jam, Master K'ung left Wey once more. Reflecting sadly on the treatment he had received at the hands of the Wey ruler, he generalized: "I have found no one who loves virtue as he loves beauty."

2. "The Master was affrighted in K'uang," says a passage in the *Analects*, IX, 5.

3. *A Stray Dog*

On his way to Ch'en, still the destination of his second trip, Master K'ung travelled through Ts'ao, Sung, and Cheng. While in the Sung capital, he had an interview with its prince, who asked him about government. After listening to the visitor's grandiloquent speech, the ruler acquiesced, but at the same time confessed that he was too stupid to put the sage's ideas into practice. There was nothing left for the Master but to leave the state.

During his brief sojourn in Sung, Master K'ung, however, had antagonized Huan T'ui, one of its powerful ministers. For three years, the Sung grandee had been building a magnificent stone coffin for himself, and while the sarcophagus still stood uncompleted, the stonecutters all fell sick as a result of the "speed-up" imposed upon them by their taskmaster. Hearing this story, Master K'ung commented caustically: "How extravagant! It would be better to let one's body rot at once."

Naturally, remarks like this took wings, and the Sung minister was infuriated at what he deemed a personal insult. Before the visiting scholar was able to leave the state line, emissaries were sent to waylay and kill him. The men of Sung overtook Master K'ung as he and his followers were rehearsing some rites under a big tree. But, being human, the pursuers could not murder in cold blood these "innocents abroad," who were peacefully engaged in the practice of ceremonies. So they just felled the tree and departed. Alarmed by the mishap, the pupils urged the Master to flee. But he said stubbornly: "Heaven has bestowed the virtue that is in me. Huan T'ui—what can he do to me?" Nothwithstanding, Master K'ung took himself off with greater precaution. Instead of going straight south, he made a detour westward to Cheng, dressed, all the way, in the tatters of a serf.

After a hazardous journey, Master K'ung arrived alone at the capital of Cheng, he and his followers having lost each other on the way. All by himself, he stood forlornly at the east gate. Upon inquiry, a man of Cheng told Tzu-kung, who had been looking for the Master, that there was indeed such a stranger at the eastern suburb with extraordinary features like those of the sage-kings of the olden days. "But," the man added, "he stood there as cast down as a dog that has lost its home." Later when Tzu-kung repeated this to Master K'ung, the sage laughed, saying: "My outward appearance matters little, but this comparing me to a stray dog—oh, how it fits! oh, how it fits!"

4. *The Sage Breaks His Oath*

Master K'ung made his first visit to Ch'en in 496 B.C., when he was fifty-six. There he settled down for some time as a minister in the court of Duke Min of Ch'en.[3] Once a wounded sparrow-hawk alighted on the ducal palace, where it soon died of the pain inflicted by a strange arrow that had pierced its body. The arrow shaft, made of k'u wood, bore a stone head one foot, eight inches long. Curious, the prince inquired its origin of Master K'ung, and straightway received a learned reply replete with antiquarian lore. The prince was especially impressed when this information was later verified by old documents found in the state archives.

But Master K'ung was not so fortunate on another occasion when he was engaged in a conversation with the Ch'en Minister of Crime. "Did Duke Chao of Lu," asked the Ch'en minister, "know the rules of propriety?" To defend the mem-

---

3. Ssu-ma Ch'ien, misreading a statement in the *Works* of Meng K'o, related that Master K'ung, while in Ch'en, dwelt in the house of Cheng-tzu, the Guardian of the Wall. This is improbable, as the "Guardian of the Wall" was an official position in Sung, similar to the Minister of Works in the other states, and Cheng-tzu could not be both a Sung official and Ch'en minister at the same time. The original passage in *Meng-tzu* therefore should be emended to read as follows: "At that time, though Master K'ung was in straits, he had as his host (in Sung) Cheng-tzu, the Guardian of the Wall, and later, (when he went to Ch'en), he was minister to Chou, the marquis of Ch'en." The marquis was posthumously honored as Duke Min. (Cf. Legge, *Chinese Classics*, II, 242.)

ory of his deceased ruler, Master K'ung replied stoutly: "Certainly, he did!" But the truth was that Duke Chao had married a daughter of the house of Wu, which had the same last name as the ducal family of Lu; and it was considered, as it still is in China today, a serious breach of etiquette for parties of the same surname to be united in wedlock. So, after Master K'ung had left, the Ch'en dignitary beckoned a pupil of the Master's to his side, saying: "I have heard that a gentleman is unbiased. But can't it be that a gentleman, too, is a partisan?" When informed of this criticism, Master K'ung readily acknowledged his error; then he added tartly: "How lucky I am! Whenever I make a mistake, people are sure to notice it!"

At this time there was a great upheaval in the southeastern part of the Chinese kingdom, hitherto dominated by Ch'u, the bear state in the southern jungles. As early as the last decades of the 6th century B.C., there had emerged from among the barbaric tribes bordering Ch'u, the two strong peripheral states of Wu and Yüeh, which were vying with each other and Ch'u to attain hegemony in the vast southern lands. For a number of years, the fertile but heretofore unexplored plains of the Yangtze valley had become a battleground of the three rival powers, with the small central states like Ch'en and Ts'ai sandwiched between the vacillating might of the contending parties. During the years Master K'ung was there, Ch'en, constantly attacked by Wu, was thus thrown into a seething sea of chaos. Feeling uneasy, Master K'ung left once more for Wey.

Fate was again unkind to the traveling scholar. Before he reached the capital, he was surrounded by the rebellious people of P'u, a border town south of Wey. But this time, instead of yielding passively to the violence of the inhospitable natives, the Lu party fought it out with their assailants. It so happened that a wealthy young man by the name of Kung-liang Ju was among the Master's retinue, with five chariots of his own. He was manly, tall, able, and noted for his bravery. He said to Master K'ung: "Sir, the last time I joined you, we were in trouble at K'uang. Today we are again in a scrape. Isn't this fate? But rather than see the Master suffer again, I will fight and die." He charged so fiercely then that the men of P'u were afraid. They said to Master K'ung: "We will set you free, if you promise not to go to Wey." Thereupon they made a sworn agreement with him and let him depart by the east gate.

In spite of his oath, Master K'ung went straight to Wey. Tzu-kung grumbled: "Can one break one's oath like that?" The Master replied: "That was an extorted oath; such a one the deities do not hear!"

5. A Bitter Gourd

When Duke Ling of Wey heard of Master K'ung's return, he was so delighted that he went outside the city as far as the open commons to greet him. He asked the Master whether P'u could be attacked. When told in the affirmative, the duke seemed pleased, but he took no action. Neither did he make use of other counsels which Master K'ung offered from time to time. An old, outworn man after more than forty years of reign and as many years of dissipation, he was too weary now to initiate any reforms, let alone those in government affairs.

It was probably about this time that an incident relating to Master K'ung's stay in Wey took place. One day, as he was playing on the *ch'ing*, a basket-bearer, hearing the music in passing, said, "His heart is full who thus strikes the sounding stone." Some time later, he added: "Oh, for shame! Why this obstinate tinkling note! If one doesn't gain recognition, why not quit at once?—that's all. 'When the ford is deep, cross it with your clothes on; when shallow, wade it with your clothes held up.' "[4]

Hearing this, the Master replied doggedly: "Where there's a will, there's a way."

4. A familiar quotation from the *Book of Poetry*, I, iii, 9, meaning "One should act according to circumstances."

But Master K'ung grew restless without employment. To be sure, he had the will, a strong, indomitable one, to achieve greatness. Under the circumstances, however, the way was not open to him. He made two desperate attempts to break from this useless inactivity which irked him, but failed in both. One time, while still in Wey, he received an urgent call from the mutinous governor of Chung-mu in the great state of Tsin. His first impulse was to go there, as he once almost did in the case of the Pi warden's invitation, but he changed his mind upon a more mature consideration. Nevertheless, when expostulated with by Tzu-lu, he protested bitterly: "Am I then a bitter gourd, good enough to be hung up to dry, but never eaten?"

According to another account, Master K'ung, finding his services no longer needed in Wey, actually went westward to Tsin. This time, his intention was to see Chao Chien-tzu, a powerful minister of Tsin, against whom the same governor of Chung-mu had rebelled. But he was again deterred from making the trip; for just as he was setting his foot on the river bank,[5] he received the tragic news that two of the noble officials of Tsin had been put to death by Chien-tzu. Fixing his eyes on the turbulent stream, the Master sighed: "How beautiful is this vast expanse of billowy water! That I shall not cross it, is fate!" Asked why he had so abruptly changed his plan, he explained: "I have heard that the sacred unicorn does not visit the countryside where people disembowel animals with young in order to slay the unborn offspring; the dragons do not bring into harmony the powers of *yin* (female) and *yang* (male) where the ponds are drained to catch fish on dry land; the phoenix does not come flying to where nests are robbed of their eggs. Why? Because every noble creature mourns the

5. The *Ho* mentioned here was usually taken to mean the Yellow River. But since both Wey and Tsin were north of the great River, it seems unlikely that Master K'ung had to cross it on his way from Wey to Tsin.

sufferings of its own kind. If even the birds and beasts shun the unrighteous, how can I do otherwise?"

After a little rest in the small town of Tsou, Master K'ung went back to Wey, where he had his last interview with Duke Ling. The aged ruler, though he now had one foot in the grave, and though he had given up all hopes of good government, was nevertheless still engrossed in military affairs. He asked the Master about battle array, and got the latter's incisive reply: "I have learned the arrangement of sacrificial vessels, but I have not learned military tactics." On the following day, Duke Ling had another conversation with Master K'ung. But instead of paying attention to the sage, he looked up wearily at the wild geese flying overhead. At this, the Master took to his heels and headed once more for Ch'en.

6. "Let's Go Home!"

Master K'ung spent his sixtieth birthday in Ch'en. Years of wandering and adversity had somehow quenched the passionate flame that once had set his heart aglow with ambition and urged him on to journey abroad to seek in other states, when his own had failed him, a prince who would lend a willing ear to his program of government reform. The dream of establishing an Eastern Chou was still temptingly intriguing; but more remote and evanescent than ever it became, as the years rolled on. Now, oftener than not, his thoughts turned back to his native land, where old ties still remained, and sweet memories still beckoned to him. Thus a message from Lu to recall one of his pupils released a flood of emotion that he had kept in check during the last few years with increasing difficulty.

Things in Lu had changed a great deal since Master K'ung had left it in angry protest at the beautiful dancing girls of Ch'i, who had monopolized the duke's attention to the neglect of his government and the disgrace of the sage-statesman. By 492 B.C., the infatuated Ting had been succeeded by Ai (B.C.

494–468), the new duke, who was now in the third year of his
reign. That same fall, Huan-tzu, the unworthy head of the
mighty Chi family, who had been the author of Master K'ung's
undoing in Lu, was breathing his last. Previously, when the
great minister was ill, he had asked to be driven out in his carriage to have a last look at the city. Looking about him, he
sighed deeply, saying: "There was a time when this state almost reached the peak of prosperity, but we never got there,
because I offended Master K'ung." Then turning round to his
son K'ang-tzu, who was following him, he continued: "Be sure
to recall Chung-ni (K'ung Ch'iu) when after my death you succeed me as chief minister."

Consequently, K'ang-tzu was anxious to fulfil his father's
last wish by summoning Master K'ung back. But one of his
retainers advised him against the move, saying: "Formerly
your father brought upon himself the derision of the princes,
when he failed to make use of K'ung Ch'iu to the very end.
Now, if you are going to engage him again, and later change
your mind, you too will be the laughing stock of the world."

"Whom, then, should I send for?" asked K'ang-tzu.

"You can call Jan Ch'iu to office."

Jan Ch'iu, a native of Lu, was at the time accompanying the
Master on his travel. When the Lu messenger came to Ch'en
with the glad tidings, there was a great stir among Master
K'ung's followers. Even the Master himself was excited. He
said in high spirits: "In recalling Ch'iu, the people of Lu are
going to make great use of him. It is not for a small job that
they are sending for him."

On the same day, Master K'ung announced to his pupils:
"Let's go home! Let's go home! The little children of my
school are getting impatient and ambitious. Though well accomplished and cultured, they still do not know how to shape
themselves."

Knowing the Master's mind, Tzu-kung went a little way

with Jan Ch'iu, as he was setting out, in order to have a private
word with him. Tzu-kung made an urgent request to his de-
parting friend: "As soon as you take office, be sure to have the
Master summoned back."

Unfortunately, long years were yet to pass before Master
K'ung was finally called home. The fault, in all likelihood,
was not in Jan Ch'iu. The officials in Lu, still remembering the
rigorous manner in which Master K'ung had purged the government of its corruption, were afraid of him; and of course,
they were jealous of his power and prestige. As a newcomer to
the official circle, Jan Ch'iu's influence was limited. He had to
wait for a favorable time when he could make good his friend's
parting wish; and that waiting, as we shall see, was a long and
tedious one.

7. Master K'ung Inquires for the Ford

Apparently not pleased with his reception in Ch'en, Master
K'ung went next to Ts'ai, a small principality west of Ch'en,
and, like it, had been a dependency of the mighty state of Ch'u.
But at this period of our history, Ts'ai had shifted its loyalty
to the rising power of Wu, and consequently had incurred the
anger of Ch'u. In the year 494 B.C., while Wu was making an
incursion into Ch'en, the army of Ch'u entered the capital of
Ts'ai. The next year, the marquis of Ts'ai, having first wept at
the tombs of his ancestors, moved his court eastward to Chou-
lai, a small city in the newly held territory of Wu.

Ill luck, it seemed, was pursuing Master K'ung everywhere
he went. It is not clear to which Ts'ai he went from Ch'en,—
whether he journeyed westward to the old site, now conquered
by Ch'u, or eastward to its new capital, where the marquis was.
Whatever the case, confusion greeted the Lu travellers as they
wandered about the devastated countryside. At Chou-lai, for
example, the marquis had just been shot to death by an unruly officer. So it is more likely that Master K'ung's destination

was the original site of Ts'ai, where those inhabitants, who had chosen to remain behind, were being deported southward to their new settlement by the Ch'u conquerors. Anyway, no matter in which direction Master K'ung might have turned, he would have found no peace or security. Nor could he find a ruler upon whose patronage he could depend for a living.

In the course of his travels, Master K'ung chanced one day upon the small fief of Yeh west of Ts'ai. There he was received by its lord, a great minister in the court of Ch'u.[6] As usual, their conversation turned to the subject of statecraft, on which Master K'ung uttered the famous dictum that "good government consists in gladdening those who are near and attracting others from afar."

Curious to know how the sage of Lu stood in the opinion of his pupils, the lord of Yeh once posed the question to Tzu-lu, but the latter refused to commit himself. Instead, he repeated it to the Master, who said: "Why didn't you tell him he is a man who forgets his food in his eager pursuit of knowledge, forgets his sorrows in its happy attainment, and does not perceive that old age is creeping upon him?"

Nothing, however, came out of this chance meeting with the Lord of Yeh. The Master continued to roam aimlessly between Ch'en and Ts'ai at a time when travel was especially difficult, for the countryside was in ruins as a result of the constant maraudings by foreign troops. Moreover, the fields had been laid waste and the people were suffering from hunger and penury. In the midst of this universal want, the Lu party

6. It is dubious whether Master K'ung met the Lord of Yeh at his fief in Yeh, or whether (according to Ssu-ma Ch'ien) he met him somewhere in the former site of Ts'ai, where the Lord of Yeh was supervising the removal of the Ts'ai people to their new home in Fu-han. But there seems to be little support for Ch'ien Mu's contention that it was in Fu-han itself that Master K'ung met the Lord of Yeh. (*An Interlinking Chronology*, pp. 44–5; "Appendix"—Table I, p. 10.) The Lord of Yeh was only one of the three officers of Ch'u in charge of collecting and selling the people of Ts'ai at Fu-han, and there was no evidence that he alone was enfeoffed there as its commander at the time of Master K'ung's visit.

found themselves out of provisions in a no-man's land. Starved and sick, they were so weakened that they could hardly stand on their feet.

In spite of this great distress, Master K'ung displayed remarkable courage and retained his composure by continuing his studies and lectures, his zither-playing and singing. But such hardships wore thin even the most dauntless of his followers. Sullen and fretful, Tzu-lu at length complained to the Master: "Must a gentleman also endure such privation?" "A gentleman," replied the sage, "stands firm in his misery. It's the small man who gives way to license in times of trouble."

Perceiving his followers' discontent, Master K'ung individually summoned three of his chief disciples, Tzu-lu, Tzu-kung, and Yen Hui, to each of whom he asked the same question: "It says in one of the songs: 'We are neither tigers nor rhinoceroses that we can stay in this wilderness.' Is my teaching false? Or why should we be in such straits here?" It was from Yen Hui, the most understanding of them all, that he got this heartening answer:

Your teaching, Master, is so extremely profound that the world can hardly comprehend it. But all the same, let's continue to extend and carry it out, no matter whether it be followed or not. Only in his determination does a gentleman distinguish himself. Yes, the fault is ours if we do not cultivate our doctrine. But if we do, and cannot get it accepted, that is the shame of the rulers. What does it matter if it is not applied!

The Master was so flattered by this observation that he smiled and said: "Ah, son of the house of Yen, if you had great riches, I should wish to be your steward!"

It is not known how the Lu wanderers finally extricated themselves from their predicament.[7] But, somehow or other,

7. Ssu-ma Ch'ien had the story that King Chao of Ch'u, hearing of Master K'ung's distress, sent soldiers to rescue him from his besiegers, and after that, Master K'ung went to Ch'u.

they managed to pull through, and secured enough provisions to proceed on their journey. Nor is it clear where they went next. Tradition has it that they travelled farther south to Ch'u, where Master K'ung made such a favorable impression on its ruler (or king, as he styled himself) that the latter was ready to enfeoff the alien visitor with a territory of 700 square li, but was dissuaded from his purpose by his jealous ministers. Soon the Ch'u prince himself died in an expedition, and with his death vanished the last great hope, if we accept the story, of Master K'ung's political advancement in a foreign country.

While in Ch'u, the Master's party had several encounters with the hermits of the southern lands, who, wearied of the riches, ambitions, and other allurements of their evil world, had retired to mountains or wilderness to commune with nature. Others turned to the good, fertile fields to draw their bodily sustenance and spiritual nourishment from Mother Earth. Still others remained in the city, where, happily oblivious of the hustle and bustle of life, they sang to their heart's content their songs of fanatical joy. Cynical, other-worldly, they were the exact opposite of the intellectual, fervent world reformers of Master K'ung's school.

One day, while Master K'ung was driving, he was greeted in song by Chieh Yü, the madman of Ch'u:

> Phoenix, O Phoenix bright,
>   Thy virtue is in decay!
> Thy future is still in sight,
>   Though the past cannot be mended.
> Up and away!
> The court is today
>   With danger attended.

About the same time, or a little earlier, Master K'ung lost his way in the country. Reaching a stream and being anxious to cross it, he sent Tzu-lu to inquire of two men working together in the fields the location of the ford.

"Who is he that holds the reins?" asked one of them.

"K'ung Ch'iu," answered Tzu-lu.

"K'ung Ch'iu of Lu?"

"Yes."

"Then he knows the ford."

Not getting the desired information, Tzu-lu turned to the other man.

"And who are you?" asked the second hermit.

"I am Chung Yu."[8]

"Follower of K'ung Ch'iu of Lu?"

"Yes."

"The whole world," remarked the hermit, "is in turmoil, and what man is he to change it? Instead of following one who flees from this man and that, would it not be better for you to choose a master who withdraws from the world altogether?"

And he went on hoeing.

Tzu-lu went back to report to Master K'ung. Sadly the Master said: "We cannot herd with birds and beasts. If not with our fellow men, with whom should I live? If everything is right with this world, what need is there for me to change it?"

On another day Tzu-lu, who had lagged behind, was looking for the Master. Meeting an old man carrying a weeding basket on his staff, he asked, "Have you, sir, seen my Master?"

"You do not toil with your limbs; nor can you tell the five kinds of grain. Who is your master?" With these words, the farmer planted his staff in the ground, and proceeded to weed.

Tzu-lu did not depart, but bowed with joined hands before the old man, who ended up by taking him home for the night. To complete his hospitality, the farmer killed a fowl and boiled millet to feed his guest; he also introduced Tzu-lu to his two sons.

The next day when Tzu-lu met Master K'ung, he related his adventure of the night before. "He must be a recluse," the

8. Chung Yu is another name for Tzu-lu, sometimes also called Chi-lu.

Master said, and sent Tzu-lu back to find him. But when Tzu-lu got there, the old man was gone.

8. *The Bird Chooses Its Tree*

After several years of fruitless wanderings in Ch'en and Ts'ai, Master K'ung returned to Wey in 489 B.C. Here political conditions were fast deteriorating. Duke Ling of Wey, who had been more interested in the flying geese than the sage's conversation, had recently died. He was succeeded, however, not by the heir apparent, who was in exile abroad because of attempted matricide, but by his grandchild, son of the dispossessed prince. This resulted in the awkward situation that Ch'e, the new duke, had to hold the country against his own father, who tarried outside with the intention of regaining his lost dukedom at any price. With the age old laws of feudal succession violated and the ties of blood relationship broken, the state of Wey was by no means the proper soil for the Master's seeds of moral and political reform.

Official opportunities for Master K'ung, however, were not lacking. Many of his students were in the service of the new duke, who hearing of the Master's great fame, was eager to enlist his support. The prince was now in the fourth year of his reign, but his position was still precarious with constant threats of seizure by his father's faction. If he could only have Master K'ung to take charge of his government, he would have a broad façade behind which to hide his unfilial conduct and a strong hand to guide the ship of state out of the impending storm.

But Master K'ung was unwilling to be involved in such a hellish mess. When asked what he would do if offered the reins of government, he answered that under the circumstances, the most urgent matter was the rectification of names. "How pedantic you are!" exclaimed Tzu-lu, who was too obtuse, despite the many years he had been with the Master, to perceive the subtle implication of this profound remark. It was apparent that he was unaware that the only way to improve the existing state of affairs was to restore the severed father-son relationship, covertly called by the Master, "the rectification of names,"—without which the government of Wey was bound to fall into ruin.

Such a recovery being impossible, Master K'ung stayed aloof from the politics of Wey. Tired of aimless wanderings, his aspirations of establishing an Eastern Chou now hopelessly gone, and the restless ambitions of his manhood no longer goading his mind, he was satisfied to lead a quiet and peaceful life in Wey, until the day, he fondly hoped, when he would be called back to his native land. This was the one last great wish to which he still tenaciously clung, the others having all vanished with the lapse of time. But Heaven being benign, Master K'ung was granted at last the desire of his heart.

Eight years had elapsed since Jan Ch'iu had gone back to Lu to pave the way for Master K'ung's return. Now such a chance finally presented itself when in 484 B.C., Jan Ch'iu, at the head of a Lu army, conducted a successful campaign against the invading Ch'i troops. K'ang-tzu, the chief minister, vastly pleased with his family steward, asked how he had attained such great military skill. Jan Ch'iu, seeing that the right moment had come, ventured a happy lie.

"I learned it," he said, "from Master K'ung."

Impressed, K'ang-tzu asked, "What kind of man is Master K'ung?"

"If you were to put him in power," replied Jan Ch'iu enthusiastically, "your reputation would spread far and wide. You would be able to apply his teachings to the people, and even the gods, whom you might consult, would not be able to find fault with them. He would strive to establish perfect moral order in the country. If you were to assign him a territory of 1000 li, he would not use it to further his own interests."

"May I then summon him?"

"Yes, you may, but you must not treat him like a common subject."

While negotiations in Lu were thus proceeding satisfactorily, things in Wey, on the other hand, were proving too unwholesome for Master K'ung's further stay. About to attack a fellow aristocrat because of a private feud, the prime minister of Wey approach^d Master K'ung for advice, but the latter turned him down with the excuse that he knew nothing about armor or weapons. Immediately afterwards, he ordered his carriage ᴜ be yoked and prepared to depart from Wey, saying: "The bird chooses its tree; but the tree cannot choose the bird."

The Wey minister tried to detain him. But just at this juncture, a group of three envoys from Lu came to Master K'ung's house with gifts of silk and an invitation to return.

After fourteen years of wandering and tribulation, Master K'ung went back to Lu, a disappointed but wiser man.

CHAPTER SEVEN

A Requiem

1. *The Elder Statesman of Lu*

THE SEXAGENARIAN SCHOLAR, WHOSE FOOTSTEPS HAD COVERED most of the central states of the Chinese kingdom, now established himself as a prodigious figure in the political circles of Lu. The fame of his success as a diplomat and judge must have suggested the fabulous to the minds of the younger generation, for they regarded him with awe and admiration. From all over the Chinese states came his great band of disciples. Some of them had already distinguished themselves as men of learning, while others held key government positions in several states. But the most wonderful of all, and the most inspiring, was the great respect, the loyalty and affection, which they displayed for their beloved Master. Here indeed was a venerable sage of supreme wisdom, whose learning was too profound to be fathomable, and whose influence, more moral than political, was too tremendous to be gauged in ordinary human terms. No private individual in these feudal times had ever before risen to such towering heights of prestige as K'ung Ch'iu when he was welcomed back to the bosom of his native land with the honor and homage befitting a returning hero.

The elder statesman of Lu, however, was not without sorrows and grievances. He was respected, to be sure, but not employed. His advice was sought and listened to with attention, but more likely than not, it was put aside as too idealistic for practical purposes. Regarding him mainly as a grand old man whom it was nice to have around for adornment and display, none of the ruling party was sincere enough to put his grandiose feudal ideas into practice. They were impatient to obtain wealth and power, but not at all concerned about the superior moral principles governing man and society, as advocated by Master K'ung.

It suffices to mention here a few instances of Master K'ung's conversations with Ai, the reigning duke, and Chi K'ang-tzu, the chief minister. To the duke's question on how to gain the loyalty of his subjects, Master K'ung answered: "Exalt the upright and discard the crooked, then the people will submit. Exalt the crooked and discard the upright, then the people will be insubordinate." Another time when K'ang-tzu asked about government, the Master observed: "To govern means to rectify. If you, sir, set an upright example, who will dare to walk crooked?"—A simple truth, but how difficult for those rulers who themselves were so crooked!

At this time, Chi K'ang-tzu was vexed by the great number of robbers that infested the state, and he desired to know what he should do to get rid of them. The Master's remedy was as easy as turning one's palm; he said: "If you, sir, were not covetous, no man would steal, though you were to reward him for stealing."

Naturally, these caustic, straightforward remarks did not gain for Master K'ung the good will of the duke or his minister. Nor would they follow his advice in important state affairs when occasionally they took their problems to him.

Immediately after Master K'ung's return to Lu, K'ang-tzu, who was instrumental in his recall, tried to use the Sage to support an unpopular measure he was about to introduce. To meet the state's expenditures and at the same time to enrich himself further, K'ang-tzu was anxious to get Master K'ung's approval of his plan to lay a new tax on the land. So he dis-

patched Jan Ch'iu to Master K'ung to press him for his sanction. But Master K'ung refused with the excuse that he knew
nothing about such things. Three times the request was made,
and three times it was rejected. Now K'ang-tzu became impatient, and sent to say: "You, sir, are an elder statesman of our
country. I am waiting for a word from you before acting on the
new measure. Why is it that you will not give your opinion?"

Still, Master K'ung refused to commit himself. But privately
he said to Jan Ch'iu: "The conduct of a princely man is guided
by the rules of propriety. In his benefactions, he prefers to be
liberal; in his actions, he observes the doctrine of moderation;
and in his taxation, he follows what is light and just. In considering the present situation by the standards of propriety, it
becomes apparent that the revenue required by the Ch'iu
ordinance[1] is more than sufficient. One who is governed by insatiable greed, even though he imposes a tax on the lands today, will still find himself in need of money to-morrow. Moreover, if Minister Chi wishes to act lawfully, there are the
statutes of the Duke of Chou; but if he wishes to act in an ir-
regular manner, what is the use of consulting me?"

The advice was unheeded, and in the first month of the next
year (483 B.C.) a new levy was imposed upon the people of Lu.[2]

An aftermath of this controversy was the abrupt alienation
between Master K'ung and Jan Ch'iu. The Master was bitter
against the oppressive law, and blamed it all on Jan Ch'iu. Ac-

1. In the first year of Duke Ch'eng of Lu (B.C. 590), the Ch'iu Chia ordinance
was passed. *Ch'iu* is a territorial designation consisting of 16 well-fields, or 144
families. But as to the exact nature of the ordinance and the number of buff-
coats (*Chia*) and other military levies such as men, war-horses, and oxen that
a *Ch'iu* was supposed to contribute under this law, scholars disagreed, and
nothing definite is known. (See Legge, *Chinese Classics*, V, 337.)

2. Legge wished that the historians who told us the origin of this tax would
also give more particulars of its enactment (*Chinese Classics*, V, 828),—a pious
wish to which we heartily concur. Unfortunately, this is impossible, and the
only thing we know on this subject is that at the time of Duke Ai, the peasants
of Lu were taxed two tenths of their produce from the fields, but the duke still
found it insufficient for his extravagant purposes. (*Analects*, XII, 9.)

cusing the latter of collecting imposts to add to the wealth of the Chi chief, who was already richer than the Duke of Chou had ever been, Master K'ung announced to his pupils: "He is no disciple of mine. Boys, you may beat the drum and assail him."

Master K'ung's last setback in the political affairs of Lu came about in 481 B.C. In that year Duke Ch'en of Ch'i was murdered by Ch'en Heng, his minister. Hearing this news, Master K'ung fasted for three days, and then, after having bathed and cleansed himself, he went to court to bring the matter to Duke Ai's attention. "Ch'en Heng has killed his prince," said Master K'ung; "I beg that you, my lord, chastise him by attacking Ch'i."

Like his predecessor, the duke was a cowardly, good-for-nothing aristocrat, who cared more for horses and women than for feudal righteousness. He answered: "Lu has long been kept in a state of weakness by Ch'i. How could we invade her as you have proposed?"

"One half of the people of Ch'i," insisted Master K'ung, "will not side with Ch'en Heng for slaying his lord. With the whole of Lu to attack the other half of Ch'i, our goal can easily be effected."

"You had better discuss this matter with the three ministers," the duke said evasively.

Master K'ung went to see the ministers, but none of them was interested in his proposal. Nor would they take any action.

Master K'ung could only console himself by saying that as an elder statesman next in rank only to the three ministers, he could not leave untold what he thought was for the best of the state.

2. *Labors of Love*

These futile political sallies were by no means the main concern of Master K'ung in the last years of his life; on the contrary, he was diligently engaged in the more congenial and constructive task of collecting and preserving for posterity the many sources of intellectual knowledge he had been imparting to his students. Having devoted almost his entire life to study and teaching, Master K'ung was now starting to gather the fruits of his labors. To this period of his intense literary activity, the world is indebted for the great Chinese Classics,[3] one of the earliest and most significant collections of literature ever compiled.

It will be remembered that at one time when Master K'ung was accused of having achieved nothing to bear out his great reputation, he had jokingly answered that he would take up charioteering or archery as a profession. But now it must have dawned upon him that he had actually accomplished little worthy of fame, and that his long life had been so far little more than a series of failures and frustrations. Of Duke Chou he no longer dreamed, as the great Duke's success in political administration was far beyond what he could ever aspire to. On the other hand, Master K'ung took consolation in the fact that his band of faithful students would hold aloft the torch of Chou culture, of which he was the Heaven-appointed, though unofficial, bearer. But something had to be done to perpetuate in writing the fundamental truths of his doctrines which till now had been only verbally expressed. Again, Master K'ung, inventive genius that he was, hit upon the idea of putting his materials together in a well-edited, definitive collection that would bear the hallmark of the school of K'ung. Thus the first of Chinese teachers became the foremost of Chinese authors.

Master K'ung's intention, however, was not so much the recording of his own ideas and interpretations of life,—such

3. I cannot agree with Fung Yu-lan's contention that the Six Classics, which Fung sometimes identifies with the Six Arts, already existed before Master K'ung's time. (Fung, *A Short History of Chinese Philosophy*, pp. 39–40.) I believe, on the other hand, that it was Master K'ung himself who put into their final shape the Classics that bear his name.

would smack of conceit and snobbishness,—as the perpetuation of that great body of ancient literature, that invaluable heritage of feudal culture, which hitherto had been in the sacrosanct keeping of the official diviners, historians, and music masters, but which now was in a state of sad neglect and in danger of perishing with the decline and fall of the states. There is no doubt that Master K'ung's decision to make a more pertinent contribution to Chinese culture by undertaking the task of arranging and editing the vast materials he had gathered for his teaching purposes was a wise one.

The general direction of Master K'ung's work of love is apparent, but it is hard in this day to determine the extent of revising and pruning which he did on the original texts. Of the Six Classics connected with Master K'ung's name, the classics *of Rites* and *Music* are now lost, the *Book of Rites* being a much later compilation.[4] The *Book* of *Poetry* as we have it today is a very remarkable volume of old Chinese poems, mostly folksongs and hymns; but here again it is debatable whether Master K'ung had only the 311 poems of his anthology to work on,—six of them were lost in the course of time,—or whether he selected these 311 out of a vast treasury of 3000 songs as reported by Ssu-ma Ch'ien.

Also doubtful is the question whether he discarded any of the historical documents when he compiled the *Book of History*. There are two possibilities here. On the one hand, it might be argued that Master K'ung would be an unworthy antiquarian, if he had mercilessly rejected any of the valuable old records from his collection. On the other, the limitations of the *Book of History* might lead one to believe that there was a paucity of Chinese historical material, which is by no

4. Though following the traditional account, I have grave doubts whether there were ever such books as the *Rites* and *Music* supposed to have been edited by Master K'ung. As for the *Li Chi,* or *Book of Rites,* now included in the K'ung Classics, it was in fact compiled much later by the Han dynasty scholars Tai Teh and Tai Sheng in the 1st century B.C.

means the case. As a matter of fact, the existence of the office of the historiographer in almost every feudal court in itself indicates that ancient China was rich in history. All in all, though we believe that if Master K'ung had been more liberal in his editorial policy, we would probably have more specimens of ancient literature to enlighten and entertain us, we are nevertheless grateful for even the scant documentary evidence of the 2000 years of primeval China previous to the 5th century B.C. that he was able to save from oblivion for the good of the entire nation.

There is likewise a great controversy as to how much Master K'ung put into the *Book of Changes,* a Chou treatise on divination and metaphysics. The conservative school maintains that he had a lion's share in the arrangement of the book, and wrote the appendices and commentaries, together with the famous ten "wings" that now bear his name. The heretics, on the other hand, deny his authorship altogether, considering all the extraneous material as forgeries by later writers. Since there is no evidence weighty enough to support or discredit either of these contentions, the whole affair becomes a happy battleground of wrangling scholars, whose weapons are mainly ingenuity plus a little dogmatism. But though we are happily non-partisan in these disputes, we are willing to assert that in his later years Master K'ung was extremely fascinated with the *Book of Changes* and read it so often that three times he wore out the leathern thongs which bound together the bamboo slips of his copy. "If a few more years were added to my life," he said happily, "I would give fifty to the study of the *Changes;* only then I might be free from grave faults."

Master K'ung's only undisputed work is *Spring and Autumn,* a chronological record of the reigns of twelve dukes of Lu, beginning with the first year of Duke Yin (722 B.C.) down to the fourteenth of Duke Ai (481 B.C.). Even here, his originality consists merely in re-arranging and revising the annual data of the Lu historiographers, to which he had access. Since the perpetuation of his grand feudal ideals was the main objective of his historical writings, he freely wielded his editorial pen to prune and tamper with the original entries, changing the wordings here and there, and sometimes even distorting the facts to conform with what he considered to be the golden rules of propriety. This classic is an avowed piece of propaganda, in which historical truth serves only as the handmaiden of moral and political beliefs. In fact, Master K'ung was so pleased with his innovations that he staked his entire fame on this single book. While delivering the revised annals to his pupils, he said proudly: "If any one in future generations recognizes my greatness, it will be because of my *Spring and Autumn;* likewise, it will be the cause of my condemnation." In the words of a later admirer, who was no less an authority than the great Meng K'o (Mencius) himself: "Master K'ung completed the *Spring and Autumn,* and the rebellious ministers and villainous sons were struck with terror."

3. *The Unicorn in Captivity*

While Master K'ung was working on his annals of Lu, an ominous event put an abrupt end to his labors. In the spring of 481 B.C., there was a great hunting expedition in the vast marshes west of the capital. A wagoner of the Shu-sun clan, while gathering firewood in the wilderness, came upon a strange one-horned animal resembling the antelope. After having broken its left fore leg in the scuffle, he captured it and took it home in a carriage. But Minister Shu-sun, who received this rare booty, considering it a bad omen, threw it away outside the suburb, while at the same time he sent a messenger to ask Master K'ung its identity.

When the Master saw the wounded animal, he burst into tears that wet the lapel of his coat. Wiping his face, he exclaimed: "Oh, unicorn, wherefore dost thou come? Wherefore dost thou come?"

"Why do you weep, Master?" asked Tzu-kung.

"The unicorn comes only when there is a sage-ruler. To see it appear untimely, and then get injured, how my heart grieves!" Thus Master K'ung bewailed his own fate, which, too, was foredoomed.

Returning home with a heavy heart, the Master wrote down the last entry on the bamboo tablets: "In the spring of the Duke's fourteenth year, during a hunt in the west, a unicorn was captured." With these words, he threw away his stylus, thus terminating, two years before his death, the chronicles of Lu.

4. Heaven Is Destroying Me!

The heart of this unicorn among men had been afflicted with sorrows that always came in droves. He had only just finished lamenting the death of his son Po-yü, who had passed away shortly after their return to Lu, when he again cried out in despair at the loss of his beloved pupil Yen Hui: "Alas! Heaven is destroying me! Heaven is destroying me!" When remonstrated by his pupils for having given himself away to such excessive grief, he replied: "Is it indeed excessive? If not for this man, for whom then should I mourn?"

But in spite of his great affection for Yen Hui, he disapproved, as unsuitable, the elaborate funeral Hui's fellow students gave him. Nor would he let his carriage be used as a hearse for his favorite disciple. It was not that he had no respect for his pupil, but that he had more respect for himself, that Master K'ung desired the use of his conveyance, saying, "Since my place at court comes after the great ministers, it is not proper that I should go on foot."

The last stunning blow came to Master K'ung when in 480

B.C., the news of Tzu-lu's tragic death reached him.[5] This brave, impetuous, big-hearted pupil of his was at the time an officer in Wey, where an armed revolt, headed by the ousted prince in an attempt to wrest the ducal seat from his reigning son, was in progress. Just as the conspirators were storming the fortified terrace of the chief minister's house, Tzu-lu arrived upon the scene. He met Tzu-kao, a fellow official and a pupil of Master K'ung.

"The gate is closed," said Tzu-kao.

"But I want to go in," replied Tzu-lu.

"It isn't your concern," said Tzu-kao; "why should you run the risk?"

"I have had my pay," Tzu-lu insisted, "and I will not flee from danger."

Tzu-kao left Tzu-lu rashly pushing his way to the gate. Once inside the minister's house, he started shouting and threatening to set fire to the terrace, where the rebels had entrenched themselves.

In the fight that ensued, Tzu-lu was beset by two of the conspirators, who, in the course of the combat, struck him with their spear, cutting off the strings of his headgear.

"A true gentleman," said Tzu-lu, the swashbuckling soldier who had become a man of ceremony, "does not die with his official cap on the ground."

Bravely he met his death at the hands of his assailants, as he was tying on his cap.

Master K'ung had predicted that Tzu-lu would not die a natural death. When he first heard of the uprising in Wey, he had observed: "Ch'ai (Tzu-kao) will come back, but Yu (Tzu-lu) is going to die." His premonition, unfortunately, was only too true.

5. A story in the *Book of Rites* says that when the messenger from Wey told Master K'ung the manner of Tzu-lu's death—"They had hewn him into pickles,"—the Master ordered forthwith that the stewed meat be tabooed from his table. (Legge, *Li Ki*, in *The Sacred Books of the East*, XXVII, 123–4.)

5. *Mount T'ai Crumbles*

The sands of time were fast running out as Master K'ung entered his seventy-third year in 479 B.C.

Rising early one morning, he walked slowly to the door with his hands behind him, trailing his staff. While he was thus sauntering, he sighed and sang:

> The great mountain crumbles!
> The strong beam breaks!
> The sage languishes away!

Having finished his song, he went into the house and sat down opposite the door. Tzu-kung, overhearing the words, said to himself, "If Mount T'ai crumbles, to whom shall I look? If the pillar falls, and the sage withers away, on what shall I lean? The Master, I am afraid, is going to be ill." So he hastened into the house.

"What makes you so late, Ssu?" asked the Master. "In the time of Hsia, the dead were dressed and coffined upon the eastern steps of the courtyard; the people of Chou kept the coffin above the western steps; and the men of Yin (Shang) placed it in the hall between two pillars. I am a descendant of Yin, and I dreamed last night that I was sitting between two pillars in front of the sacrificial offerings." Then he continued: "Since no intelligent king has risen, who under heaven is there who will take me as his master? My end, I fear, is near."

Master K'ung took to his bed, and died a week later on the *chi-ch'ou* (11th) day of the fourth moon in the sixteenth year of Duke Ai of Lu, and concurrently the forty-first of King Ching of Chou (479 B.C.).

6. *The Last Obsequies*

The death of Master K'ung was an occasion of great sorrow in Lu. The venerable statesman, whose counsels were unheeded during his lifetime, was heaped with eulogies. Now that he was dead and could no longer enjoy them, innumerable honors were showered upon him.

Duke Ai even mourned Master K'ung's death in an elegy:

> Merciful Heaven, no compassion showest thou!
> The grand old man thou wilt not allow
> To live, to guard me, the Unique One, on my seat!
> In grief I mourn, my sorrow is complete.
> Woe is me! O woe! O venerable Ni![6]
> Gone art thou who wast a monitor to me!

It is hard to gauge the sincerity of the duke's sorrow, full of conventional sentiment as the poem is. But Tzu-kung criticized it on the grounds of propriety. "Our lord," he observed, "is certainly not going to die in his native land. The Master once said: 'The want of propriety makes one dull-witted; the improper use of terminology leads one astray.' When one loses his will, he becomes besot; likewise, when one does not face the right direction, he goes astray. It is contrary to the rules of decorum to eulogize after his death a man whom one was unable to use when living. In calling himself 'The Unique One' he was presumptuous. In both the prince has erred."

The disciples were anxious to give their revered Master a grand funeral according to the best in feudal tradition. Fortunately, there was among their number a Kung-hsi Ch'ih, a ceremonial expert in the K'ung school. Since ritual was his speciality, the greatest ambition of Ch'ih's life, so he had told his Master, was to be clad in a black robe and a linen cap, and assist in a small way in the services of the ancestral temple. And the Master had remarked: "If Ch'ih were to play a small part, who would there be to play the leading one?" Because of this qualification, Kung-hsi Ch'ih, we can well imagine, was unanimously chosen to take charge of the rites at Master K'ung's funeral.

After the eyes of their dead Master had been sealed, three

6. i.e. Chung-ni, Master K'ung's literary name.

pinches of rice were sprinkled in his mouth; then he was dressed in a complete ceremonial robe with a full dress-cap and a precious jade ring, attached by a cord woven of twisted threads of different colors. Thus arrayed, the body was placed in a double coffin, its inner chest of t'ung wood and outer shell of pine being respectively five and four inches in thickness. The whole was then adorned in the style of Chou, with a wall-like curtain and fan-shaped screens; above them all was spread a rich canopy of tooth-edged pennants after the manner of Yin; while long streamers of white silk floated aloft on flag-staffs in the tradition of Hsia. Thus were the best features of the three early dynasties combined and consummated in this grand funeral for the greatest of all teachers of ancient rites.

Master K'ung was buried north of the Lu capital on the bank of the river Ssu.

At first the pupils were perplexed about their dress on this sad occasion. Then Tzu-kung said: "When Yen Hui died, the Master wailed for him as for a son, but he wore no mourning clothes. He did the same in the case of Tzu-lu's death. I suggest that we too bemoan the Master as if he were our father, but not wear any mourning dress." His fellow students most probably acquiesced. But even so, some of them, to express the depth of their affliction, did not remove their sackcloth headbands when they went out of the house.

Master K'ung's disciples mourned him for a period of three years. After their mourning was over, they packed their luggage and made ready for home. As they were taking leave of Tzu-kung, who alone chose to stay longer, they wailed together so long that they all lost their voices. Then each went his own way.

Tzu-kung was so devoted to his master's memory that after seeing the others off, he went back and built himself a mud hut beside the burial mound, where he remained for another three years.

CHAPTER EIGHT

There Is No Class in Education

1. *A Transmitter of Ancient Lore*

The story of Master K'ung's life, such as we have just narrated, bears witness to the fact that he was foremost of all a great and well beloved educator. This is shown in the sincerity and depth of feeling with which his students mourned him after his death. As a statesman, he met with varied and uncertain success, but as a schoolmaster, he won the love and admiration of his contemporaries as well as of posterity. It is fitting, therefore, that we begin our study of Master K'ung by stressing his role as a pioneer in the teaching profession and his contribution to the educational history of the world.

In the first place, Master K'ung was a zealous student, a devoted scholar, and an indefatigable pedagogue whose popularity lay chiefly in his ability to cultivate a perfect personal relationship with his pupils. Mild yet majestic; awe-inspiring yet not fearsome; respectful, yet easy and composed; Master K'ung was to the younger members of his big academic family a revered and affectionate parent, whose words were treasured and obeyed. In their daily contacts with this transcendent spirit, they were inspired by his integrity, his devotion to learning, the extent of his knowledge and the depth of his wisdom. Willingly they submitted to the magnetism of his personality; gladly they trod in his footsteps; eagerly they perpetuated his teachings. Only in this way was the rich lore of ancient China, of which Master K'ung was the personification, preserved for posterity.

Above everything else, the Master was, as he said of himself, a transmitter of knowledge, a believer in and lover of antiquity. We have already seen how in the last years of his active intellectual life, he was engaged in his labor of love, putting into their final shape those works of literature which were henceforth to be known as the *Six Classics*. These were the source books of the school of K'ung, upon which he had based his articles of faith, and from which he had gathered his fund of wisdom. "I was not born," he said, "with knowledge; I simply love the past and am earnest in its study."

This early passion for learning kindled the latent sparks in Master K'ung's soul. There are frequent references to his forgetting food in the eager pursuit of knowledge, his gaining relief from sorrows and troubles in the joy of its attainment. To him, one of the pleasures of life was to learn, and then to review constantly what he had learned. Without eating or sleeping, he used to spend whole days and nights in meditation, often with no results. Then he would go back to study again. And it was an arduous, enthusiastic study, always seasoned with the apprehension of his never being able to catch up with it, that finally brought to him the happiness of fulfilment and enlightenment.

"In a hamlet of ten families," said Master K'ung, "there must be men as faithful and true as I am, but none as fond of learning." The Master, we know, was not in the habit of exaggerating his own merits. In another passage, his characterization of a scholarly gentleman best describes the Master himself: "A princely man does not seek satiety in his food or comfort in his home, but is earnest in his business and cautious in his speech, and seeks the company of the righteous for the rectification of his conduct. Such a person may rightly be said to be in love with learning."

To be able to acquire new knowledge, while thinking over the old, qualifies one as an instructor of men. Such a teacher was Master K'ung himself. "What do you find, indeed, in me?" he asked; "a quiet brooder and memorizer? an insatiable learner? an unwearied monitor of others?" The answer to this rhetorical question is that Master K'ung was all three; but it was especially as an unwearied tutor that he gained the love of his students and the admiration of all. In moments of humility, he would deny in scholarly fashion that he possessed any true erudition. Then he would add naively: "But if an ignorant fellow from the lower classes should come to me with a question, I would discuss the subject from beginning to end, and set it fully before him."

He believed that in education there was no class distinction.

2. *Three Corners of a Subject*

Though tremendously serious in teaching, Master K'ung had little of the pedant in his make-up. He was against mere memory work which hampers freedom of thought. He was not interested in training men whose one ambition is to be able to answer queries and quizzes. Nor was he interested in satisfying the curious by ransacking old books and documents for out-of-the way, believe-it-or-not information. On the other hand, his method of instruction was, what we would call, highly inspirational.

As the Master himself said, he would not open the door of knowledge to any one not eager to enter; nor would he expound the dictum of truth to students incapable of forming their own ideas. "Nor," he continued, "have I anything more to say to those who, after I have made clear one corner of the subject, cannot deduce the other three." But he had not praise enough for the intelligent pupil, who, as in the case of Tzu-kung, when given a clue, was able to find the way, or who, like Tzu-hsia, knew how to interpret the Master's remarks which were always so pregnant with hints and suggestions. It was only after the student had proved his intelligence in this way, he maintained, that he was ready to start on poetry.

The Master was also convinced that a little learning is a dangerous thing; so is knowledge unattended with careful deliberation. "Study without thought," he observed, "is labor lost; thought without study is perilous." As an orthodox exponent of ancient culture, he was opposed to the infiltration of outlandish doctrines, which he asserted to be injurious.

The Master further maintained that from learning, that is, the attentive contemplation of the material and spiritual world, comes knowledge, which is synonymous with comprehension and wisdom. But a man should also have a clear, honest view of his intelligence. He must recognize his own limitations. "Yu," the Master said to Tzu-lu, "shall I instruct you what knowledge is? When you know a thing, to hold that you know it; and when you do not know a thing, to allow that you do not know it,—this is knowledge."

According to Master K'ung, a scholar should be familiar with three things, namely, the decree of Heaven, propriety, and language. Mere understanding is useless, while knowledge, on the other hand, should be followed by the selection and application of what is good. He said: "There are those who act without knowing why. But I am not like that. To hear much and then to select the good and follow it, to see much and then to ponder on it—this comes next to true knowledge."

The most essential study, however, is the study of man himself. One of the disciples once asked Master K'ung about the great virtue called *jen,* or "human-heartedness." "It is to love humanity," said the Master. Then the disciple asked

again about knowledge. "It is to know humanity," was the
Master's answer.

Truly has Master K'ung said: "Grieve not that men do not
know you; grieve that you do not know men."

3. Individualized Tutorship

The basic principle of Master K'ung's educational program
is this: "By nature men are nearly alike; but through experience they grow wide apart." While men are much alike at
birth, it is their lives and the habits they acquire that make
them different. And one of the chief factors that differentiates
one man from another is knowledge, which is essentially moral
in its transforming effect. So thought Master K'ung; and a
matter of great regret it is that instead of learning for one's
self-improvement, as did the ancients, people nowadays learn
with a view to approbation alone.

The Master held moreover that this kind of ethical education should be inculcated in varying doses according to individual needs and capacities. One of the secrets of Master
K'ung's success as a teacher was the intimate knowledge he
had of his students; he was familiar with their shortcomings
as well as their talents. He knew them better than a father his
sons, or an executive his employes. He made a careful study
of their problems, interests, and character with a view to
shaping them into a perfect pattern. A good illustration of
the high quality of his individualized, custom-tailored tutorship is to be seen in the following anecdote typical of the
schoolroom of K'ung.

When Tzu-lu asked whether he should immediately put
into practice what he had learned, the Master told him that
while his father and elder brothers were still alive, he should
not act rashly but consult them. The same question was posed
by another student, Jan Ch'iu. But this time the Master gave
exactly the opposite advice: Yes, he should immediately ex-

ecute whatever he had learned. Kung-hsi Ch'ih, the ritualist, who had overheard both conversations, was puzzled by the apparent inconsistency of the Master's replies to the two inquirers. Repeating the discrepancies, he continued: "I am perplexed, sir, and venture to ask for an explanation."

"Because Ch'iu is diffident," Master K'ung happily assured him, "I urged him forward; because Yu is overconfident, I held him back."

Unlike many of the dogmatic, conceited old pedagogues that followed him, Master K'ung had a high opinion of the younger generation knocking at his school gate. To be sure, to those who made no name for themselves at the ripe age of forty and fifty, no respect was due; they would carry their mediocrity to the grave. But a young man, said Master K'ung, is greatly to be feared. "Who knows," asked he, "but that the future generation will surpass the present?"

Noteworthy also is the fact that in his teaching, Master K'ung was impartial. He treated his students as if they were all his children, and he gave each the same training he gave his own son. Once Ch'en K'ang, one of his pupils, plagued by a suspicion that the Master might have privately favored Po-yü with special instructions, seized an opportunity to quiz the Master's son: "Have you learned anything different from what we all have had?"

"No," answered Po-yü; "but once as I was hurrying across the hall, where my father was standing alone, he said to me, 'Have you learned the odes?' 'Not yet,' I replied. 'If you do not know them,' he admonished, 'you will have no hold on words.' I retired and studied poetry. On another occasion, as he was again standing by himself, I hurried across the hall to greet him. 'Have you learned the rituals?' he asked. 'Not yet,' I replied. 'Without learning them,' he said, 'you will not be able to establish yourself.' So I retired and studied the ceremonials. Only these two things have I heard from him."

Ch'en K'ang was delighted at this revelation. He said to himself as he left his fellow student: "I asked one thing and got
three. I have learned about the odes and the rituals; and I
have learned too that a gentleman is reserved towards his son."

4. In the Schoolroom of K'ung

Since the Master was liberal in his educational policy and
by no means snobbish in his attitude towards students, all
types of eager-eyed, wide-mouthed young men were admitted
to the portals of his lecture hall. They came from every part
of China, but mostly from Lu, Wey, Ch'en, Ch'i, Ts'ai, and a
few from the peripheral states of Ch'in, Ch'u, and Wu. Ssu-
ma Ch'ien has recorded, no doubt from hearsay, that all in all,
Master K'ung's pupils totaled 3000. Even though this may be
a gross exaggeration, the number of his followers must have
been considerable, for we can still name today seventy or more
of the Master's chief disciples.

The average student came from the middle-class *shih*
family, as did Master K'ung himself, but there were also rich
scions of noble clans with chariots and attendants of their
own, and plebeians of peasant stock, who brought to the Master the humble tuition of a bundle of dried meat. To all and
sundry, if they were earnest in their search for knowledge, the
Master gladly imparted his instruction. The only distinctions
he ever made were those of the learner's mental capacity and
industry. "The best men," the Master said, "are born with
knowledge. Next come those who learn to know; then the
others who, though dull and slow, are nevertheless willing to
be instructed. As to those stupid ones who yet refuse to learn
—they are the lowest of all." In the realm of education, Master
K'ung reasoned, there is an aristocracy of intellect and a
nobility of character, but socially speaking, all men are born
equal and should be treated as such.

The ages of Master K'ung's pupils varied greatly. Tzu-lu,

one of the senior disciples, for example, was only nine years younger than the Master himself, whereas Tzu-chang, the last to join the great academic circle, was forty-eight years younger.

There are also two intriguing instances of father and son going to school together under the tutorship of Master K'ung. Interestingly enough, in both cases, it was the junior who outshone his father in intelligence and scholarship. Yen Hui, whose early death was greatly lamented by his fellow students, was noted for his devotion to learning, while Tseng Ts'an,[1] the other young man, was one of the chief heirs to the cultural legacy of the school of K'ung.

Besides the six arts which comprised the chief training of a Chou aristocrat, Master K'ung further offered his followers instruction in belles-lettres, and the conduct of life, faith, and truth, the last three being entirely ethical in nature. Here again we can see the Master's stress on morality as an essential part of a gentleman's education. The four major departments of study in which his students specialized were ethics, rhetoric, statecraft, and literature. Generally speaking, while moral uplift was the main concern of all, the art of government and the art of speech, both indispensable for diplomatic intercourse, were the chief interests of the earlier pupils, many of whom aspired like the Master to high government positions and ended up by becoming state officials, stewards of the great families, and magistrates of baronial cities. On the other hand, the group of younger men, as they gathered around the Master in his last days in Lu, distinguished themselves in the fields of literature, philosophy, etiquette, and music. Whereas most of their senior colleagues were men who possessed high executive abilities, this class of neophytes became accomplished scholars and thinkers, who brought to fruition the moral, political, and cultural teachings of their Master.

1. The word *ts'an* is also pronounced as *shen,* and Tseng Ts'an is often referred to as Tseng Shen.

5. *"Let Each of You Make a Wish"*

Unlike the southern hermits, who with their other-worldliness faced life with scepticism and disillusion, Master K'ung taught a philosophy of life that was strikingly of this world. In morals and politics, he was an ardent reformer; and though he might have sinned on this side of orthodoxy, even his conservatism was not unredeemed by his shrewd commonsense. He was essentially a teacher of the art of good and wise living, who demonstrated to his students by words as well as deeds how to make the most of one's life by herding with one's fellow men and performing faithfully one's duties towards society. A good illustration of this aspect of Master K'ung's teaching is to be found in a conversation he had with Yen Hui and Tzu-lu, who happened at the time to be waiting on him.

"Come," said the Master, "let each of you make a wish."

"I should like to have," said Tzu-lu, "carriages and horses, and robes of fur to share with my pals, and I would not regret if we should wear them out together."

"As for me," replied Yen Hui, "I should wish to make no boast of my talents, nor a display of my good deeds."

Then Tzu-lu turned around to the Master, saying: "Now we should like to hear you make a wish, sir."

"It is my wish," the Master replied, "to nourish the old, to cherish the young, and to be true to friends."

It was indeed as a moral man and social reformer that the Master had posed. In fact, this was the goal towards which he had directed all his political efforts, however meager the rewards had been. But his appearance, like that of the unicorn, had been untimely, coming as it had after the general dissolution of the feudal system. Thus had resulted the greatest conflict in the Master's mind, in which he was divided between his life-long desire and determination to improve the lot of his fellow men on the one hand, and on the other, an ever growing realization that all his exertions in this direction were doomed to failure, as at one time or another he ran into the blind alley of politics, where his head was frequently bumped in the darkness, and his feet were sore from bootless trudging.

It is no wonder, then, that there were fleeting moments, in which Master K'ung felt gloomy and wished to retire altogether from this naughty world. One moment he yearned to embark on the vast, unknown sea; the next, he was so disgusted with civilized life that he even entertained the wish of making his home among the nine wild tribes of the east.

"They are barbarous," someone objected. "How could you live with them?"

"Where a gentleman has his home," replied the Master, "what savagery could there exist?"

Of course, he never actually carried out his threats. But often, because of his disappointments, this most ambitious of mortals had to be resigned to the unexciting and simple life of the average man of the countryside. "With coarse rice to eat," he said, "with water to drink, and a bent arm for a pillow— herein lies true happiness. Ill-gotten riches and honors are to me like a fleeting cloud."

Not that the Master was unmindful of power and rank, which he certainly pursued during all these years of his active life, but to acquire them by unrighteous means was to him worse than not having them at all. Even then, he did not shun them like a viper and might have fallen into the snare, set by the rebellious governors of Pi and Chung-mu, had it not been for his better judgment and Tzu-lu's protest.

6. *Singing in the Spring Breeze*

In view of our last observation, let us now take a good look at the schoolroom of K'ung, where an extremely charming picture presents itself. Here we see the Master in the midst of his students, Tzu-lu, Tseng Tien, Jan Ch'iu, and Kung-hsi

Ch'ih,—a congenial group, though their interests and talents vary,—relaxing after a heavy schedule in a happy discussion.

"Forget for a moment," beams the Master, "that I am a day or two older than you. Let us suppose that at present you are out of work and feel that you are not appreciated. Then some one comes along who wishes to use you; what employment would you choose?"

Impetuous Tzu-lu is the first to make answer. "Give me," he boasts, "a state with a thousand chariots, hemmed in by powerful neighbors, overrun by invading armies, with famine and drought to boot, and I could in the space of three years teach its people courage and propriety."

The Master smiles.

"What about you, Ch'iu?" he asks.

"If I had charge," replies Jan Ch'iu, "of a territory of sixty to seventy square li, or one of fifty to sixty, I would in three years' time give its people plenty of food and provisions. As to rites and music, I'd wait for a superior man."

"How about you, Ch'ih?"

"I wish merely to speak of the things I wish to learn," answers modest Kung-hsi Ch'ih, "not of the things I can do. In the ceremonies at the ancestral temple, or in a gathering of princes, I should like most of all to be dressed in the straight robe and official cap of the junior assistant."

"What about you, Tien?"

Tseng Tien, the last of the four to be called upon to tell his life's ambition, has all this while been playing on his zithern. Its tinkling notes now linger and then gradually die away in the tranquil study hall, as he pushes his instrument aside and rises to reply. "I fear my choice cannot compare with those of the other three," he ventures timidly.

"What harm is there in that?" says the Master. "I just want each of you to speak his mind."

Then says Tseng Tien: "On the last day of spring, clad in spring clothes, with five or six newly capped youths, and six or seven lads, I should like to bathe in the river Yi, and fan myself with breezes from the rain-altars. We would then return home singing."

At this the Master heaves a sigh, saying, "I am with you, Tien."

CHAPTER NINE

The Master and His Pupils

1. *An Ornate Temple Vessel*

MASTER K'UNG'S SUCCESS AS A TEACHER LIES MAINLY IN HIS FEL-
lowship with his pupils. A congenial and convivial atmosphere
pervaded the schoolroom of K'ung. Though the Master was
outwardly reserved and dignified, there were moments when
he relaxed in the company of his faithful disciples. It was then
that he shed the cloak of formality and revealed the warmth
of his inner self in little pleasantries and caresses, rude rebuffs,
and angry denunciations. An entirely different person from the
rigid, ceremonious prig that he appeared to be when in attendance at court, he became at such time a most amiable and com-
panionable person, his cup of life filled to the brim with the
milk of human kindness. It is indeed in his varied and conflicting moods, in the cross-currents of emotion surging beneath
an unruffled surface of propriety, in the antithetical trends of
his personality that baffled analysis, that we discover the real
K'ung Ch'iu, the historical schoolmaster of Lu, who was just
as human as any of us.

From a number of schoolroom conversations and anecdotes
we catch intimate glimpses of the personal relationship between the Master and his motley band of aspiring students.
Let us record a few more of them.

The Master's humor was at its best in the witticisms

he directed at his students. In Lu, a sheep offering used to be made in a temple ceremony at each new moon to invoke sanctions from the spirits. The rite, however, had been sadly neglected by the duke, though as a mere formality, the sheep was still offered. Since its original spirit was lost, Tzu-kung, the economist, proposed to do away with the sacrifice altogether. But Master K'ung bantered him, saying: "Ssu, you grudge the sheep; but I love the rite."

At the same pupil Master K'ung directed another of his witty sallies. Tzu-kung was in the habit of making comparisons between people. "How splendid is Ssu!" exclaimed the Master. "But as for me, I have no time for such things."

Lest the reader should mistake the Master's real opinion of this talented pupil, whose devotion to the Master was great, and whose eloquence excelled even that of his teacher, we hasten to add that their relations were most satisfactory. In fact, the Master had many kindly words for Tzu-kung, and once compared him to a rich sacrificial vessel adorned with precious stones—a very high compliment indeed. It happened like this. At the time Master K'ung was commending another student for his gentlemanly conduct. Hearing the praise, Tzu-kung asked: "And what do you say of me?"

"You are a utensil," said the Master.

"What kind of utensil?"

"An ornate temple vessel."

2. A Martial Tune on a Scholar's Lute

Another butt of Master K'ung's devastating raillery was Tzu-lu, the converted swashbuckler who stood out from among the scholarly group for his dashing manners and courage. Only a few years the Master's junior, and a life-long follower, he would sometimes take liberties with his mentor, as we have seen in a previous narrative. While frank and straightforward, he was also, as once stigmatized by the Master, "untamed." He never slept over a promise, and, to quote the Master again, "could settle a litigation with half a word." Too rash to be thoughtful or imaginative, and possessing a rudeness that was provokingly attractive, he was nevertheless a most likable character.

Master K'ung was fond of making fun of Tzu-lu. He once told his students that, since his teachings were making no headway, he would like to board a raft and go drifting on the sea. Then he added: "And who would follow me but Yu?" Hearing this, Tzu-lu was glad; whereupon the Master said: "Yu is more venturesome than I, but he lacks judgment."

On another occasion, when Tzu-lu was playing a martial tune on the "scholar's lute," the jumbling notes of his music jarring the tranquillity of the peaceful schoolroom, the Master complained: "What business has the lute of Yu to twang at my door!" This slighting remark spread so fast that Tzu-lu's fellow students began to show him less respect than was due a senior member of the school. Seeing this, the Master immediately counterbalanced the unhappy effect of his inadvertent words by a compliment: "Yu has climbed to the hall, though he has not yet passed into the inner chamber."

Tzu-lu's worth, however, was not unrecognized. Son of a poor couple, he had had in his early days herbs and pulse for food, while he had fed his parents with rice carried home on his back for more than a hundred li.[1] Ever since then he had shown a brave contentment in poverty, for which he had won the Master's praise: "Dressed in a tattered robe quilted with

1. The story of Tzu-lu's filial devotion is told in the *Twenty-four Cases of Filial Piety* as follows: " 'Alas!' said Chung Yu, 'although I was a scholar, yet my parents were poor; and how was I to nourish them?' Exhausted, he travelled the long road and cheerfully brought rice for his parents. Pleasantly he endured the toil and exerted his utmost without any commendation. At that time his lot in life was hard and unfortunate, and he little expected the official honors he afterwards enjoyed. But when his parents were dead, and he had become rich and honorable, enjoying all the luxuries of life, then he was unhappy and discontented, not as cheerful as in the days of his poverty, nor happy as when he ministered to his parents' wants."

hemp, yet standing unabashed side by side with those clad in furs of fox and badger—who elso could have done it but Yu?" Master K'ung also had a high opinion of Tzu-lu's purity and fidelity. "Since I have had Yu," he said, "no bad words have entered my ear."

On his part, Tzu-lu was entirely devoted to his Master, equally ready to argue with him, to be snubbed by him, and to fight and pray for him. In the last instance, Master K'ung once declined his student's service as shown in the following episode.

Once when the Master was sick, Tzu-lu asked leave to pray for him.

"Is this the custom?" asked the Master.

"Yes," answered Tzu-lu. "It is written in the *Eulogies*:[2] 'Pray to the spirits in Heaven above and on earth below.'"

"Long have I prayed." With these words Master K'ung graciously dismissed his pupil's good but useless intentions.

There is another moving scene between the ailing sage and his devoted disciple. One time Master K'ung again fell seriously ill, and Tzu-lu engaged his fellow pupils to simulate stewards to minister to the Master's needs. By this feigning he fondly hoped to comfort the sick old man with an illusion of his former grandeur as a great minister of state. But instead of approbation, Tzu-lu brought upon himself the Master's scorching rebuke. When during a conscious moment, Master K'ung became aware of the deception practised on him, he called his students together to his bedside, saying: "Long has the conduct of Yu been deceitful! By pretending to have stewards when I have none, whom shall I deceive? Shall I deceive Heaven? Moreover, rather than die in the hands of serving men, I would much prefer to breathe my last in the arms of

2. Probably a Litany or Eulogy of the Dead. Legge wrote in his note to this passage: "Tzu-lu must have been referring to some well-known collection of such prayers." (*Chinese Classics*, I, 70.)

you, my boys! And though I may not get a grand funeral, am I to die by the roadside?"

The Master, as we have seen, actually survived Tzu-lu, who got killed in an uprising in Wey a year before Master K'ung himself passed away.

3. He Is Ofttimes Empty

Surrounded by such a galaxy of talented followers, the Master, apparently, found it hard to be unbiased. His great affection went especially to Yen Hui, the most intelligent as well as the most industrious of all. With such a brilliant and promising young scholar as Hui, what teacher could refrain from showing partiality?

In concise, graphic words, Master K'ung once made a very interesting comparison between Tzu-kung and Yen Hui. "There is Hui," he said, "who has attained. He is ofttimes empty. As for Ssu, he will not bow to fate, but hoards up his substance. In his calculations he seldom makes a mistake." Here is a clear picture of two entirely different personalities: the one, a born financier, who later became a reputed millionaire of the time; and the other, a devoted student of the truth, without any worldly ambitions and vanities.

For Yen Hui, the Master had nothing but high praise. In an understatement characteristic of a Chinese schoolmaster, he observed that "Hui was not stupid," but a quiet, reflective student, who listened attentively to the lectures for a whole day without making any show of smartness by raising hair-splitting arguments on what he had heard. But this did not mean that Hui was a dullard, for as soon as the session was over, he would engage in deep contemplation until he was able to expound and illustrate the teachings of wisdom.

Moreover, this attentive intellectual was also diligent and hard-working. His devotion to study is proverbial and an object of emulation among Chinese scholars. The Master said further of Yen Hui: "I have not yet heard of any one who loves learning as he does." Again he remarked: "Never listless when spoken to—such is Hui."

This inborn intelligence and industry, coupled with his great love of learning, made Yen Hui the best of scholars in this greatest of all schools. But this is not all. The Master's favorite was also an epitome of virtue. He never repeated a fault; he never lost his temper. According to the Master, for three months together he was able to keep his heart free from any thought that deviated from the true path of virtue; while the others might "hold out for a few days, or a month at most, but no more." Because of his poverty, Yen Hui's virtue was especially praise-worthy. "How admirable is Hui!" exclaimed the Master. "Living in a low alleyway with only a bamboo bowl of rice and a gourd cup of water, no ordinary man could have endured such misery. Yet mirth never failed Hui."

No wonder the Master was unconsolable when Yen Hui's life was cut off in its prime, shorn of the chances of fruition of his flowering genius. For such a perfect student the following words of the Master would serve as a fitting epitaph: "Alas! I have seen him advance, but never have I seen him halt in his progress."

4. *The Filial Trio*

After Yen Hui's premature death, the onerous duty of carrying out and extending the Master's teaching fell at length upon the shoulders of one, who, ironically enough, had first given Master K'ung the impression of being "dull-witted." This, however, was not a matter for surprise, for Tseng Ts'an, one of the younger students to join the great school, was a poor lad from the country at the time of his presentation to the august Master, and as a young man certainly did not distinguish himself among his contemporaries. Nevertheless, this "dull-witted" scholar rose to distinction as the most learned and revered of all the disciples. The reputed author of *The Great Learning*,[3] one of the four influential books of the classical school, Tseng Ts'an won eternal fame by giving a final interpretation to the fluent oral traditions imported by Master K'ung.

Tseng Ts'an's speciality was ethics, especially in the field of filial piety, of which he was the most perfect example as well as the greatest exponent. Like many of Master K'ung's pupils, as we mentioned before, Ts'an came from a poor plebeian family. His father Tien, obviously of an artistic, carefree temperament as we have learned in a previous narrative, had left home long before to study under Master K'ung, leaving his wife and son in great poverty. A bond of sympathy, electric in nature, soon developed between the mother and son. One anecdote has it that one day when Ts'an, a lad of fourteen at that time, went to gather faggots in the hills, he was suddenly seized with a gnawing pain in his heart. Knowing that his distress had some connection with his mother, he dropped his bundle of firewood and hastened home to find out what the matter was. His mother was evidently expecting him, for she told him that, greatly perplexed by the news that guests were coming to their home from a great distance, she had leaned against the door post and gnawed her fingers. "I bit them," she said, "in order to summon you to return."

In later life, so far did Tseng Ts'an carry his filial devotion that he divorced his wife for having served up a poorly cooked pear to his mother. He never married again.

Besides Tzu-lu and Tseng Ts'an, we must also name Min Sun among those of Master K'ung's disciples who were outstanding examples of filial piety. These three, in fact, are often spoken of collectively as the famous filial trio. Having lost his mother in early youth, he lived with his father and a

3. Tseng Ts'an's authorship of the *Great Learning* has been disputed by modern scholars. (See Hughes, *The Great Learning & The Mean-in-Action,* pp. 100–4.)

stepmother, who had two children of her own. While they were clothed in warm padded gowns, Sun had only a thin garment made of rushes. Driving his father to town one severe winter morning, he was so numbed with cold that he dropped the reins from his hands. For this carelessness, he was unjustly flogged; but he made no complaint. Afterwards, when his father discovered the shabby treatment his second wife had given to his eldest son, he was so angry that he wanted to divorce her. But Min Sun pleaded for her. "Whilst mother remains," he argued, "one son is cold; if she goes away, three sons will be destitute." Touched by these words, the stepmother reformed, and the fame of Min Sun's virtue spread far and wide.

For his wisdom, as for his filial conduct, Min Sun gained Master K'ung's profound respect. "That man seldom speaks," the Master said, "but when he opens his mouth, he is sure to hit the point." He was also one of the disciples whose manners gladdened the old schoolmaster's heart. In contrast to Tzu-lu's martial gait and Tzu-kung's genial affability, Min Sun's manners were marked by polite restraint. With pupils like these, what teacher would not be pleased?

Another trait that distinguished Min Sun was his indifference to official preferments. In this respect he was unlike his ambitious colleagues. When asked by the Chi family to be warden of their city Pi, he declined the offer, saying to the messenger: "Kindly make some excuse for me. But if any one comes with a second invitation, I shall have to retire to the banks of the river Wen."[4]

5. *Rotten Wood Cannot Be Carved*

In the great school of K'ung, as in any other school, there were bound to be some who did not come up to the Master's expectations. To these black sheep the severe mentor gave no

4. Wen is a river that divides Lu from Ch'i as mentioned in page 79.

quarter. We remember how he assailed Jan Ch'iu for collecting oppressive taxes from the people; and how he branded another pupil, who had asked about farming, a mean little fellow. His greatest fury, however, fell upon Tsai Yü, a student of literature and language, who was careless about the conventions. A dissenter from the orthodox school. Tsai Yü rebelled especially against the Master's insistence on the three year period of mourning after the death of a parent. Considering so long a period detrimental to the practice of ceremonies and music, as well as a good life in general, he proposed to shorten it to a year. But Master K'ung snubbed him with the reply that a gentleman would act quite differently.

"Would you feel at ease," the Master took Tsai Yü to task, "in eating good rice and wearing silk brocade?" (That is, after only one year of mourning.)

"Yes, quite so," answered Tsai Yü defiantly.

Dumbfounded by this bold statement, the Master could hardly contain his anger. "Well," he railed, "if you feel this way, just go ahead. But a true gentleman in mourning does not relish the dainties he eats, derives no pleasure from the music he hears, and feels ill at ease in his comfortable home. That is why he abstains from such things. But if you are happy in them, you may do as you please."

After Tsai Yü left, the Master accused him before his fellow students: "How heartless is Yü!"

But it was not only his open revolt against the prescribed rites, but also his incorrigible habit of falling asleep during the Master's lectures, that Tsai Yü incurred Master K'ung's greatest displeasure. If the Sage could not stand the Wey duke's staring at the wild geese during their conversation, still less could he endure such lack of respect and attention in his own classroom. His denunciation of this delinquent student on this score was unusually furious and forthright. "Rotten wood cannot be carved," fumed the red-faced Master, "nor can a wall of dried dung be trowelled. This Yü—what's the use of my denouncing him any more?"

Another time he said: "In my early dealings with men, I used to listen to their words and take their deeds on trust. Now it is my custom to give ear to what they say, and then keep a watchful eye on what they do. It was my experience with Tsai Yü that brought about this change."

Extremely rare were these stern moods compared with the numerous pleasant and tender moments the Master usually enjoyed with his students. But of sorrows he had plenty in his last years as, one by one, his scholars dropped from the tree of life like immature fruit in a dry spell. We have already seen with what vehemence he bewailed the death of Yen Hui and Tzu-lu. It suffices now to show the Master in his role of a loving, grieving teacher. When Po-niu, another favorite disciple, was sick in bed with a mortal disease, Master K'ung went to see him. Without entering the patient's room, he grasped the withering hand through the window, exclaiming: "It's all over with him! This is fate! Alas, that such a man should have such a sickness! That such a man should have such a sickness!" The intensity of the Master's grief overcame the restraint of these poignant words. It was the one discordant note that jarred, alas too often! the happy serenity of the school house of K'ung.

6. *Few Have Gained the Gate*

If the Master was very critical of his students, the latter were full of veneration for their great teacher, of whom they spoke in the most rapturous and enthusiastic language. Not a word of disparagement, except for a few dissenting notes from Tzu-lu, was ever heard; on the other hand, they joined their voices in paeans of love and praise.

The most eloquent testimony to the profundity of Master K'ung's teaching was made by Yen Hui, the most learned of his disciples, who, while grieving for his inability to comprehend it, happily admitted that the Sage's wisdom was too alluring to be withstood. "The more I strain my gaze up towards it," said Yen Hui, "the higher it soars; the deeper I drill down into it, the harder it becomes. One moment it appears before me; the next it is behind. Step by step the Master skilfully lures me on. He has broadened my mind with culture and curbed my conduct with ceremony. And now, even though I want to stop, I cannot. After having exhausted all my abilities, I seem to see something stand out in front of me, sharp and clear, but while I long to pursue it, the way is closed."

In the judgment of his disciples, the Master was incomparable in virtue as in wisdom. Among the innumerable epithets they used in describing him are: mild and temperate, courteous and complaisant, dignified and deferential, all of which add to his summum bonum. To his followers he was as unattainable as the heavens approached on a ladder; he was as insurmountable as the sun and moon that hang high in the firmament. To disparage him was therefore like decrying these heavenly bodies. Indeed, to him no harm could come, however sharp the arrows of malice, which would bound back with a vengeance on the slanderous bowman himself. Whoever criticized the Sage would only reveal the smallness of his own soul and an ignorance of his own capacity.

Tzu-kung, for instance, objected vigorously when told that he was superior to his great Master. Since he knew that this was impossible, he made a very good case in his protest. "Let me," he said, "take as an example the palace walls. My wall reaches only to the shoulders. Peeping over it, you may see the pretty houses and homes within. But the Master's wall rises so many times a man's height that no one, who is not let in by the gate, can have a good look inside at the beauty of the ancestral temple and the rich array of its hundred officers."

Then he added: "Few indeed are those who have found the gate!"

CHAPTER TEN

The Golden Thread

1. *"Not Knowing Life, How Know Death?"*

WE HAVE ALREADY MENTIONED THE DIFFERENT SUBJECTS THAT were taught in the K'ung schoolroom and the many talented young men who gathered there to be trained in the genteel manner of a Chou aristocrat. Such being the main purpose of Master K'ung's teaching, it was natural that ethics and politics should be the two main topics of conversation that animated his lecture hall. The Master was a traditionalist, a transmitter of antiquarian lore, a fervent upholder of Chou feudalism as instituted by the renowned Duke; but, above all, he was an original thinker who derived from his contemplation of the past fresh ideas for the improvement of his own society. And wasn't it true, moreover, that the great pedagogue, who possessed profound knowledge and an inexhaustible fund of wisdom, was also the greatest teacher of life in all its kaleidoscopic aspects?

In Master K'ung's scheme of life, only a small corner was reserved for religion. Of course, he was neither agnostic[1] nor irreligious. He did not repudiate the gods and spirits of his people, but showed a sympathetic understanding of the religious faith of his forefathers as a part of their high moral endeavor. He often spoke of Heaven as an all embracing Provi-

1. Hu Shih, as well as many other scholars, maintains that Master K'ung was agnostic. (See Hu Shih, *The Chinese Renaissance*, Chicago, 1934, p. 81.)

dence, regarding himself as its instrument on earth, a wooden bell to arouse the people from their lethargy. He respected spiritual beings and insisted on preserving the elaborate sacrificial rites, especially the cult of ancestors. In accordance with the saying, "Worship the spirits as though they stood before you," he would worship them with great sincerity and reverence. "If I am not present at the sacrifice," said Master K'ung, "it is as though there were no sacrifices at all."

On the other hand, in spite of what has been said, Master K'ung was in no sense a religious teacher, and least of all, the founder of a religion like Jesus or Mahomet.[2] He made no claim to Heavenly descent or divine revelation. He worked no miracles; he unravelled no mysteries. He was against spirit-mongering, for among the subjects on which he did not discourse were ghosts, prodigies, and disorders of nature. Thus, while honoring supernatural beings, he "kept aloof from them." In accordance with this attitude, he avoided committing himself on any theological question. He refused to be wafted on the wings of metaphysics to the realm of the Great Unknown, where only pure ideas exist. In reply to Tzu-lu's inquiry on how to serve ghosts and spirits, the Master remarked: "If we fail in our duty to the living, how can we serve the dead?" And when Tzu-lu asked about death, the Master's answer was: "Not knowing life, how can we know death?"

These golden sayings contain eternal truth. By turning the human mind away from all speculative, celestial concerns, and by discouraging men from a vain search for that dark, unfathomable domain known as death and the even more mysterious region of life-after-death, Master K'ung, the supreme humanist, taught his followers to take a more realistic interest in this present life, teeming with the Creator's own crea-

2. It is regrettable that too much has been made of Master K'ung's "faith" by those religion-complexed missionaries of the early days. Some of them went so far as to insist that the K'ung dogma was a religion, and Master K'ung its founder. Nothing, of course, can be further from the truth.

tures and bustling with their myriad activities. Well has the English poet said:

> Know then thyself, presume not God to scan;
> The proper study of mankind is man.

While refusing to scan the Divine by climbing the dizzy heights of imagination, Master K'ung kept an intent eye on man's earthly ties and ethical relations. Not through fear of punishment and hope of reward in another life did he exhort men to be good. Virtue was to have its own reward, and so was life, for life's sake in this mundane sphere.

2. *The Noble Man and the Little Fellow*

In order to understand Master K'ung's moral code, we must first examine the feudal foundation upon which he built his doctrines. It has been pointed out that at the beginning of the Chou era, a wide gap had separated the two main classes of society,—the aristocracy and the peasantry, and that the gulf had been somewhat bridged over by a new middle class comprised of the dispossessed aristocrats, the rising *shih* class, and a prosperous group of merchants, artisans, and private landowners. In the meantime, the old distinctions of birth began to give way to the more fundamental distinctions of intelligence and education, and a lesser noble like K'ung Ch'iu could aspire to be, and did become, a high official and an honored guest in the court of princes. Thus with the gradual disruption of the social order there came a corresponding change in social conceptions, from which there finally evolved a new ethics for all classes of men.

Take, for instance, the evolution of the word *chün-tzu*, which we have previously discussed. While an interesting philological study in itself, the change was also illustrative of the manner in which Chinese ethical ideas were being reshaped in the course of centuries. The "lord's son," a typical

aristocrat, was now divested of his hereditary glamor and transformed into a "man of virtue" without any reference to his
station in life. He was still a gentleman, to be sure, but one
who did not necessarily descend from some great family with
blue blood in his veins. Likewise, *hsiao-jen,* originally the word
for peasant, came to mean a low, despicable person with only a
slight tinge of his rustic origin. In both cases, ethics triumphed
over feudal distinctions,—a remarkable achievement, for
which the credit went to Master K'ung.

Even then, the change was not as complete as we might
imagine. There still remained traces of the original meaning
in the new interpretations given by Master K'ung. The most
instructive example is to be found in his remark that "while
chün-tzu cherishes virtue (or personality), *hsiao-jen* cherishes
the soil; and while *chün-tzu* loves punishments, *hsiao-jen*
thinks only of favors." The whole passage is unintelligible unless we view it in the light of the historical origin of the two
key words. *Chün-tzu,* who was here the noble overlord,[3] derived an ample income from his lands; not having to worry
about a living, he was duty-bound to cherish virtue with
which to rule his subjects. On the other hand, *hsiao-jen,* the
commoners, set their heart on the soil, because as serfs they
drew their sustenance from Mother Earth. Moreover, the
aristocrat, who had the sanction of law on his side, had the
authority to administer penal codes to the little fellows, who
could only hope for favors from their superiors in the forms
of amnesties, immunities, exemptions, and what not. A vivid
picture of feudal society came to life in these words of Master

3. The use of the word *chün-tzu* as a noble overlord went back to the days
of Duke Chou (12th century B.C.). In an address to his son Po Ch'in, whom he
was sending to Lu to be its new ruler, the great statesman-father exhorted: "A
chün-tzu does not forsake his kinsmen, nor offend the great ministers through
neglect. Friends who have long been in his service he does not dismiss without
grave cause. Nor does he seek in one man talent for every employment." (*Analects,* XVIII, 10.)

K'ung, who was simply stating an historical fact without attaching to it any moral significance.

In other passages, Master K'ung, while using the word *chün-tzu* in its feudal sense, enriched it at the same time with its new ethical connotation, so that the two began to merge imperceptibly into one. In one of his sayings in the *Analects*, Master K'ung listed four virtues of a *chün-tzu*: "He was courteous in his private conduct, punctilious in serving his master, kind in his dealings with the people, and just in exacting services from them." From this, it is obvious that one of *chün-tzu's* duties was to serve his superior, the prince, from whom he received his land and his authority over the peasants. But a *chün-tzu*, too, distinguished himself by his private as well as his public virtues. In fact, the universality of his character was such that it completely overshadowed the particular attributes of his class. Once an ideal aristocrat, he now became an ideal gentleman.

At the hands of Master K'ung, nobility of birth gave place to the more pertinent nobility of character, which to him was all that mattered. Starting with a body of moral precepts intended for the aristocracy alone, Master K'ung, the great humanist, ended up by establishing a new code of ethics for all humanity. The old ideals of a Chou prince thus became the prevailing ideals of a princely man, to be observed and cultivated by all. And it was by transplanting feudal conceptions into a universal ethical system that Master K'ung made the greatest contribution to Chinese thought.

3. *The Metamorphosis of* Li

Another word that underwent an enormous change is *li*, in which is embodied the essence of Chou culture. Originally a set of sacrificial rites practised by the noble lord as head of the family and ruler of a state, it came to include, as we have noted, all kinds of non-religious observances on the great occasions of life such as capping, marriage, and mourning; it included, too, ceremonies observed in feasts, archery contests, and meetings of the feudal princes. In all these rites, a *chün-tzu,* or an aristocrat, had to be well tutored so that he would not by his rude manners become a laughingstock in polite society. While the penal code controlled the actions of the humble folk, *li,* that great body of feudal regulations, governed the conduct of the ruling class. It instituted the proper forms of princely intercourse as well as rules of religious worship, whereby a feudal lord presented himself to the spirits of Heaven and Earth; it also instilled a sense of piety and respect in the minds of the nobility.

As a teacher, Master K'ung was versed in the rituals, not only of Chou, but also of the two earlier dynasties of Hsia and Shang. Of these remote times, he could still describe the ceremonies, though he deplored the lack of literary evidence to support his words. But it was the more "elegant and complete" ceremonies (*li*) of Chou, that great conglomeration of ritual, etiquette, and culture rolled into one, that especially captivated the great pedagogue.

Master K'ung, however, was not content with presenting mere ceremonials and rules of proper conduct for the upper class. While conducting a thorough investigation into the underlying spirit of *li,* he made a happy discovery of the ethical substructure, upon which these ceremonies were founded. Stressing the principle rather than its appurtenances, Master K'ung believed that no rites should be performed without due regard to their moral implications. "A man without virtue," he said, "what has he to do with rites? What has he to do with music?" Again he protested: "Ceremonials! Ceremonials! Do they mean no more than offerings of jade and silk? Music! Music! Does it mean no more than bells and drums?"

When asked about the fundamentals of *li,* a big question indeed, the Master answered: "In ceremonials at large, it is better to be sparing than extravagant; as for mourning rites, there should be deep grief rather than minute attention to details."

Let us take, for example, the three years' mourning for parents. A typical product of the feudal age, it was designed primarily for the rich idle noble, who could afford an elaborate funeral, as well as the leisure for such an extended period of bereavement. But for Master K'ung, it meant more than a mere feudal practice. While giving these ancient observances his sanction, he also tried to find out the psychological basis, the raison d'etre of such a time-honored practice. And he found it in the sentiment of filial piety, that loyal devotion a son bears towards his parents; he also found it in the deep, inconsolable sorrow one feels upon the loss of one's beloved. "Only when a child is three years old," said Master K'ung, "does he leave his parents' arms; so must three years' mourning be the universal mourning period everywhere below heaven."

Master K'ung's new philosophical findings gave a fresh lease of life to these out-worn feudal ideas and customs. Originally a code of ritual for the privileged few, *li* was now transformed into a set of general rules of propriety, the regulating principle in any well-ordered society, be it feudal, monarchical, or democratic. Instead of being regulations of a nobleman's conduct, it became the regulations of a man's noble conduct.

As taught by Master K'ung, a *chün-tzu* should be modest and spotless in his private conduct, just as he should be courteous and observant of the proprieties in his public relations. In another statement, the Master observed that a *chün-tzu* was one who made righteousness his first principle and performed it according to *li*. "He is modest in bringing it (*li*) forth and sincere in carrying it to completion. Such indeed is a princely man!" In other words, *li* is the chief instrument whereby man attains perfection. Its pervading influence is everywhere in his moral life, while without it all the great virtues would go astray and get lost in a sea of confusion,—thus courtesy would become tiresome, caution turn to timidity, courage to unruliness, and uprightness to harshness. Well did the Master say that *jen*, the supreme virtue, consisted in "submitting oneself to *li*." And when asked for an explanation, he continued: "Look not at what is contrary to *li*, listen not to what is contrary to *li*, speak not what is contrary to *li*, and make no movement that is contrary to *li*."

The transformation of *li* was now complete. No longer a mere pattern for aristocratic conduct, it became the prime motivating force in a great ethical system that governs the conduct of all men. Great is *li!*

4. *One Thread Runs Through Them All*

This brings us to the essence of Chinese ethics as taught by Master K'ung. One day when Master K'ung was conversing with Tseng Ts'an, he remarked casually: "Ts'an, there is one thread that runs through all my teachings."

"Yes," answered Tseng.

After Master K'ung had left, the disciples crowded around Tseng Ts'an to find out what the golden thread was that wove together the Master's ethical teachings.

"Our Master's doctrine," said Tseng, "is simply this: *chung* and *shu*."

*   *   *   *   *

The Chinese word for *chung* is made up of the components "middle" and "heart." With one's heart in the very center, neither to the left, nor to the right, one will be able to achieve *chung*, which is faithfulness to one's self, to one's own nature, and to the humanity that is in one. Only then can one be faithful to one's fellow men, as shown in the virtue of *shu*. This great word has the meaning of "as one's heart," that is, "to do to others as your heart prompts or urges you." It is fellow feeling, or consideration for the feeling of others; above all, *shu* is altruism: to cherish the other's heart as if it were one's own.

Once Tzu-kung asked: "Is there a single word that one can live by all one's life?"

"Is not *shu* such a word?" said the Master. "Do not do to others what you do not want done to yourself."

5. *Human-Heartedness and Human Relationship*

In our opinion, however, *chung* and *shu* are only two of the main ingredients of *jen,* the supreme virtue frequently mentioned by Master K'ung. A composite of "two" and "man," *jen* stresses the relationship between man and his fellow men. The word has been variously translated as love, charity, benevolence, sympathy, humaneness, humanity, true manhood, and the like. Not satisfying wholly any of these restricted meanings, *jen* is probably any one or all of them. For lack of a better rendering, we have accepted the awkward but freshly-coined term, "human-heartedness," as its nearest equivalent in English. What is interesting to note is that both *chung* and *shu,* which have their root in the human heart, meet and unite in this all-embracing virtue of *jen.* It is, in fact, the very thread that strings together all of Master K'ung's ethical teachings.

For *chün-tzu,* the superior man, *jen,* is the supreme virtue. Without it, a *chün-tzu* is no longer a *chün-tzu;* he is unworthy of such a name. "Not even for the space of a single meal," said Master K'ung, "should a *chün-tzu* act contrary to *jen.* He is never so harried, never so tottering, but that he cleaves to it." Master K'ung also said that "the way of a *chün-tzu* is three-fold. Being human-hearted, he is free from anxiety; being wise, he is free from perplexity; being brave, he is free from fear." An interesting question is whether Master K'ung himself possessed these attributes of a *chün-tzu.* Very modestly he admitted that he fell short of this ideal, but Tzu-kung, who overheard the remark, insisted that the above was exactly a picture of the Master himself.

Though a supreme moral principle, *jen* is not hard to attain. "Is *jen* indeed so far away?" asked Master K'ung. Then he answered himself: "I want to have *jen,* and lo! here it comes." In other words, his doctrine of *jen,* being devoid of abstruse qualities, is a practical morality within the grasp of all. It hangs aloft on the tree of life like ripe fruit, and one has but to reach the branches to pluck it.

To be more specific, *jen* is the virtue of being courteous in private life, politely attentive in business, and honest in all human relations. "And," the Master added, "it should never be abandoned even though one goes to live amid the barbaric tribes of the east or north." This saying of the Master is significant both for the fairness of its application and the breadth of its scope. Virtue is virtue indeed when it transcends the barriers of race, creed, and time.

As a natural feeling that comes directly and spontaneously from the human heart, *jen* is incompatible with any artificiality or falsehood. "Clever words and flattering looks seldom speak of *jen,*" so warned Master K'ung. On the other hand, the supreme quality of *jen* is to love humanity and to serve one's fellow creatures, not by insinuating looks, but by deeds and example. "A man of *jen* is one who, in seeking to establish himself, finds a foothold for others, and who, desiring attainment for himself, first helps others to attain. To be able to take one's own feelings as a guide in dealing with others is indeed the direction of *jen.*"

The basis of *jen,* essentially a man-to-man relationship, is to be found first, according to Master K'ung, in one's duties towards one's parents and brothers. Fraternal love, which Master K'ung characterized as mutual friendship and joyful harmony, was often mentioned together with filial piety. Friendship too was highly regarded by Master K'ung as a basis of *jen*. To him, one of the good things in life was to have many worthy friends, and one of the greatest pleasures, to have guests from afar.

As to the relations between man and wife, Master K'ung had very little to say, and the little that he did say was no credit to him. He accused women, together with *hsiao-jen*, the low class people, of being difficult to deal with,[4] for he said, "If you are intimate with them, they do not respect you; but if you keep them at a distance, they resent it." This lack of understanding of women on the part of Master K'ung is one of the weak links in his ethical system; it is also the one place in which he failed to rise above the feudal mentality of his age.

Filial piety, we must stress, was the cornerstone of Master K'ung's ethical teaching. Built on the foundation of the patriarchical family, where the father ruled supreme, filial piety required great sacrifices on the part of the children. But Master K'ung was able to inject into it a human element that somewhat modified the rigidity of the feudal pattern in the Chinese family. He said, "Sons nowadays merely support their parents. But even dogs and horses can do that. Without a feeling of respect, what is there to distinguish men from beasts?"

When asked about the meaning of filial devotion, Master K'ung replied laconically: "Never disobey." But what or whom should one never disobey? As was his habit, Master K'ung delighted in making his students ponder over the meaning of his statements, until the truth became clear. But to make sure that his listeners were not misled, he finally explained: "While parents are alive, serve them according to *li*. When they die, bury them and sacrifice to them according to *li*." So

4. Quite a few English translators of the *Analects* (Legge, *Chinese Classics*, I, 194; Lyall, *The Sayings of Confucius*, p. 98; Soothill, *The Analects of Confucius*, p. 199, etc.), who must have had difficulties with their domestics during their stay in China, very appreciatively represented the Master as saying that maids or servants (i.e., *hsiao-jen*) are "hard to train," "to behave to," or "to keep in the house." The mistake is due to their ignorance of the historical origin of the word *hsiao-jen*.

after all, Master K'ung was not teaching blind obedience to one's parents; what he taught was the noble conduct of life that requires reverence towards our elders, whether they are living or dead.

Master K'ung's rule for filial conduct is found in the following vague, but thought-provoking, remark: "Behave in such a way that your father and mother will have no anxiety about you except your health."

To present more concretely Master K'ung's teaching on human relationship, we quote: "A youth should be dutiful at home, and fraternal when abroad. He should be earnest and sincere; he should be overflowing in love for all, while cultivating the friendship of the virtuous. If, when all that is done, he still had any energy to spare, then let him study the polite arts."

6. *Virtue Always Has Its Neighbors*

Master K'ung was a past master at wise sayings. Though living in a feudal age some 2,500 years ago, he sounded the note of wisdom and uttered dictums of golden truth that have retained their brilliance in spite of time. In the course of centuries, dynasties have risen and fallen, mores and fashions have changed, and even the powerful and long established family system has tottered with the collapse of the old social structure. But man's inherent moral nature abides as the one constant factor in a sea of changing values. With his mature experience and deep insight, Master K'ung knew exactly of what stuff man was made, and how man's life could best be improved. Here then we find the Master at his best. Unaffected by class consciousness and social inhibitions, he was able to teach untrammelled the art of sane living.

Like his elder contemporary Lao Tzu, Master K'ung often spoke of *tao,* a way of life. But the word, as he used it, is essentially ethical in meaning, denoting the principle of truth, particularly, the right way of living. Of this ethical *tao*, Master K'ung was a devoted student, and he confessed that he would be content to die the day he learned it. To know *tao*, however, is not as good as to love it, and to love it is not as good as to practise it; for notwithstanding its loftiness, *tao* is attainable, and man alone has the capacity and the volition to accomplish it. Man, in fact, is the master of *tao*, for "a man can enlarge the way, but there is no way that can enlarge the man."

The way, of course, leads in many directions. To begin with, one should do what one perceives to be right, while the omission of it is a sign of weakness. One should cultivate his talents; and rather than worry about his lack of fame, a gentleman (*chün-tzu*) should be distressed by his lack of ability. Moreover, he should be careful of his speech, for he who boasts too much will find it hard to make good his words. He must think deep and look far into the future. As the Master said, "Without giving thought to the future, one will have troubles at home." Or, to put it differently:

> He who cares not for the morrow
> Will soon have his sorrow.

Another word commonly used by writers of Master K'ung's period is *teh*, a man's moral force or character. If *tao* leads the way, *teh* follows with its host of virtues. A very famous saying of the Master's is "Virtue dwells not alone, but will always have neighbors." Of these, we have already discussed such typical ones as "human-heartedness" (*jen*), righteousness (*yi*), loyalty (*chung*), and altruism (*shu*). It suffices to mention here the two negative virtues, patience and restraint, that also figure so largely in Master K'ung's ethical system. While he maintained that the self-restrained seldom erred, Master K'ung also said that those who lacked forbearance in small matters would make a mess of greater projects.

As we have already seen, by relegating intellectual activities such as the study of the polite arts to a secondary position, Master K'ung stressed moral cultivation as the chief concern of life. But man, though a moral being, is also a social animal in his relations with his fellow men. Hence, in line with his ethical teachings, Master K'ung asserted that an individual could gain through his human contacts an infinite fund of wisdom to improve and enrich his life. First of all, a man should demand much from himself, but little from others, so as to eliminate any ill-feeling or conflict that might arise from expecting too much. Next, he should be constantly alert in his dealings with people. While he must avail himself of every chance for self improvement through contacts with a worthy man, he should also guard against wasting his time with the unworthy. "Not to speak to one with whom you can converse with profit, is to lose him," said the Master; "to speak to one who is not worthy to be talked to, is to waste words. He who is truly wise never loses his friend; he, too, never wastes his words."

According to Master K'ung, we can always find in a party of three a teacher whose good qualities we should emulate and whose bad qualities we should avoid. In another passage, the Master tells us: "When you meet a man of worth, think how you may attain to his excellence. When you meet an unworthy one, then look within and examine yourself." In other words, self-examination, which enables us to find out our faults with a view to mending them, is a necessary part of a man's endeavor; yet it is only when we have first seen these faults mirrored so unflatteringly in others that we come to realize how equally ugly ours are.

7. The Flowering of the Individual

All in all, we should say that the secret of Master K'ung's success as an ethical teacher lies in the practicability of his teaching. Without getting involved in metaphysical speculations, he set forth clear and concrete rules of conduct capable of application in daily life. He formulated no theory of the universe, and he did not even bother about the theory of knowledge, which to him was only a means towards the end of moral cultivation. In fact, he did not even philosophize on a good way of life, but taught by words that were intelligible to the average man, and precepts that were easy and simple to follow; he too possessed a personal appeal that went directly to the heart of his listener.

With an eye on man's social relations, Master K'ung worked out a practical scheme, wherein humanity could herd together in peace and concord. The large family, to be sure, would still remain the basic unit of society, but he recognized that in this close-knit and multi-celled organism, man is indisputably the nucleus, the center of myriad activities. It is he who, after cultivating his own person, brings about harmony in the family; it is also he who, after the families are regulated, creates order in the state and peace everywhere below heaven. No matter from which angle we view it, the individual man is, after all, the hub of the universe.

In other words, while thinking primarily of the feudal society of his time, Master K'ung discovered by a happy stroke of genius the ethical individual. Neither innovator nor revolutionary thinker, he had gone back for his moral inspiration to the feudal standards of the early days when the privileged aristocrat had governed and acted according to a fixed code of conduct. But as a result of his deep understanding and his ready response to fresh ideas, the ritual expert soon turned a moral reformer, and the advocate of aristocracy became an instructor in noble living for the common man. And from this seething activity in his mind there emerged the brave new concept of the individual, hitherto entirely ignored, but now recognized as an important member of the community, which depended on him for its success. No longer just one of the milling masses in a primitive society, without character or personality of his own, individual man was now exalted to his new position as a social entity, and then schooled for his part in life in the principle of moral conduct and human relationship. Besides, he was also taught his true worth, irrespective of birth or rank, his unassailable position in society, as well as his duties in the family and his relation to his fellow men.

Thus for the first time in the history of man, the dignity of the individual was asserted, his rights and obligations defined, and his moral integrity stressed, so that "from the Son of Heaven down to the common people there is unity in this: that for everybody the flowering of the individual is to be one's ultimate aim."

CHAPTER ELEVEN

To Govern Means to Rectify

1. *A Good Feudalist at Heart*

IT MAY SEEM STRANGE THAT MASTER K'UNG, THOUGH THE MOST prominent teacher of his time, never came to be a tutor of princes. Most of the young men who went to him for instruction in government came from poor or middle class families, and ended up as stewards of great ministers or commandants of outlying towns. But Master K'ung himself was not without experience in politics. In the course of his travels, as we have related above, he had on several occasions been called upon to advise rulers on state affairs. When in Lu, he was also engaged in administrative tasks that had given him firsthand knowledge of the actual workings of the government. All these experiences had contributed much to his political philosophy, which was to go down into history as the most important influence in this field during the last twenty centuries or more.

But unfortunately for posterity, Master K'ung's interest and viewpoints were confined to those of a particular class, the ruling aristocracy. Except for his early experiences as a petty official, he had had few dealings with the common people, and very rarely would deign to converse with them, as in the case of the peasant woman at her son's grave, which occasioned the Master's famous remark on oppressive government. Even then, if we are to believe in the anecdote, he himself did not speak to the woman, but sent Tzu-lu as his interlocutor. Though a dispossessed noble on the borderline between aristocracy and commonalty, Master K'ung was not only patrician in his habits and manners, his food and dress, but also in his attitude towards the common folk, for whom he had nothing but indifference and contempt, and occasionally, condescension.

Far from being the revolutionary thinker that he was recently dubbed by an American scholar,[1] Master K'ung was a conservative, an upholder of orthodox traditions. In the field of ethics, to be sure, he did emerge triumphant from class distinctions. His human touch on feudal materials was the magic touch that made all that glittered gold. But he was less fortunate in his political theorizings. A good feudalist at heart, Master K'ung based his teachings on the assumption that a golden age of order and prosperity had existed in the early days of the Chou dynasty, and that the confusion in his century was largely due to an unhappy deviation from the feudal norm, to return to which, consequently, was the most urgent of all political needs. This time-worn structure, he knew, was in the process of crumbling, but he also believed that it was not too late to repair and prop it up, so that the restored edifice might yet weather the storms of many a future generation.

Thus, with great quixotic zeal, Master K'ung set out single-handed on his self-appointed mission of restoring feudalism. But what could he do? With what could the tottering system be renovated? The "rectification of names" was the pedagogue's happy answer.

1. See Creel, *Confucius, the Man and the Myth,* of which the central theme, it seems, is that Master K'ung was a revolutionary reformer of his period. Reformer he was in a certain sense, but it is doubtful whether Master K'ung was ever a revolutionist even after Creel's very scholarly arguments and the many evidences he introduced in support of his thesis. My main contention that Master K'ung was a champion of feudal ideals, as the readers can easily see, is entirely different from Creel's.

2. *The Doctrine of Rectification*

The restoration of the decadent feudal regime through the use of correct names! How pedantic it sounds, as it certainly was!

But Master K'ung had his reasons.

The specific occasion of his remark, as the reader may recall, was a question from Tzu-lu about what Master K'ung would do if he were given the reins of government in Wey. In the light of the political situation in that state, with the prince fighting his exiled father and the ministers usurping the powers of their ruler, the Master's words were particularly significant and revealing. But they too had a more general application. As Master K'ung himself put it: "If names are not correct, then words are inappropriate; when words are inappropriate, then things cannot be accomplished. Then rites and music will not flourish, punishments will not be properly awarded, and the people will not know where to put hand or foot. Hence a *chün-tzu* designates what can be properly stated, and speaks only of what can be properly executed. In what he says, there will be nothing that is remiss."

In this sense, the rectification of names is much more than a mere point of terminology, or the correct use of language, but the first principle of morality. As such, it also provides a clear definition of one's status in society, while it gives at the same time an implicit ethical judgment on a person by the title he bears. To rectify the names is therefore to set up an objective standard of values, of right and wrong, noble and mean, high and low. And by stressing the need of correspondence between the actualities of life and the names given to them, it demands that each individual behave in strict accordance with what the name of his position implies. Thus a ruler should act like a ruler, a minister like a minister, and everybody his particular part in society. Furthermore, the rectification of terms is also a powerful weapon of stabilization with which to combat changes, to prevent the existing order from being undermined by giving it a logical foundation. When this is accomplished, it would then be possible for a prince always to remain a prince, a minister always a minister, and a subject always a subject; thus peace and order would prevail in the state.

A noteworthy attempt in this direction is to be found in the *Spring and Autumn*. It is obvious that here Master K'ung was not writing a history,—since there were already many such works by historiographers in each feudal court,—but applying to historical records his principle of rectification. On the one hand, he endeavored to give the exact meaning and relation of each word in his chronicle, using only the proper word for the proper occasion; on the other, he distinguished and rectified the rank of each feudal lord who appeared in his pages. The usurping kings of Ch'u, for instance, were given their original title of viscount, with which their ancestors had been enfeoffed. And when the Chou sovereign was summoned to a conference of the feudal lords at Ho-yang by the hegemonist Duke Wen of Tsin, Master K'ung, to whitewash the indignity, wrote that the Son of Heaven had gone there for a hunting expedition. By a careful choice of words, Master K'ung also indicated his praise or censure for each historical figure. It is interesting to note in this connection that in recording the 36 instances of the murder of a prince in the period covered by his annals, Master K'ung worded each act differently to express his judgment on it. By thus manipulating historical facts, he succeeded in creating an illusion that the entire Chou aristocracy was moving regularly in its orbit, though the atrocious deeds perpetuated by its individual members, even Master K'ung, the great apologist, could not very well conceal. What he could do, as he himself said, was to use history as a warning to the rebellious ministers and wicked sons of the future.

To Master K'ung, the principle of rectification did not end with historical writing, but should be extended to politics as well. No doubt he thoroughly enjoyed a good pun when he remarked that *cheng* (to govern) was *cheng* (to rectify). But at the same time, he must have seriously believed that the art of government consisted mainly in putting things right. A sound doctrine indeed! The big question was, however, who was to be responsible for this great task? Naturally, the prince and his ministers. For, asserted Master K'ung, if the prince himself were upright, he would be able to govern his state well. Indeed, who would dare walk crooked, when the ruler led his people along a straight path?

In the last analysis, what Master K'ung taught was essentially a body of precepts for governing the common people from the viewpoint of the hereditary ruling class, to which he was attached, and with whose interests and privileges he identified himself. The doctrine of rectification was therefore merely a conservative idea that Master K'ung advanced to reinforce the crumbling feudal structure at a time when it was in imminent danger of being undermined by revolutionary forces from without.

3. *A Paternal Government*

In spite of what has been said, there were redeeming features in Master K'ung's political doctrine. Though he was bound, as we have seen, by the fetters of time and class, which he could hardly break through, Master K'ung nevertheless contributed to feudal politics by advocating a personal approach to it. A great humanist at heart, he looked at all political problems from a human angle and based all his judgments on a human standard. He demanded in turn that government should be conducted for the sake of humanity.

The blending of ethics and politics in Master K'ung's system was natural enough when we consider the source from which he derived his teaching, and the manner in which he conducted it. It was plainly from the moral codes originally intended for the feudal lords (*chün-tzu*), and now used to teach his students, that Master K'ung evolved his ethic-politico system. It especially laid stress on the good behavior of the ruler as a prerequisite for successful government. Indeed, as we shall soon discover, this basic conception gave unity to the entire body of Master K'ung's teachings.

Just as Master K'ung's ethical ideas germinated from the ceremonial practices of the aristocrat and developed into the flowering of the individual, so did his political thoughts spring from the feudal soil and grow into the three branches of the ruler, ministers, and subjects. Their interlinking relationship fascinated Master K'ung and provided him with the key to the knotty problems of the state. To his great satisfaction, he found the solution in the management of a big family.

The state, according to Master K'ung, was just a family writ large. The prince was the patriarch of the clan; the ministers, his stewards; and the people, his dependents. Such probably was the origin of the state in its very primitive stage, when a close relationship existed between the ruler and the ruled. As we have noted before, in a simple feudal society, the feudatory had direct contact with the peasants, who rendered him service in return for his favors and protection, matching his benevolence with their loyalty. In the earliest days, the feudal government had been a personal government; most probably too, it had been an ideal government as Master K'ung asserted that it was.

Though the small fiefs had outgrown their original size and developed into big sovereign states, in which the machinery of government was much more complicated, Master K'ung still thought that it was possible to return to these model states of the early days. In his yearning for the idealized past,— for once, the practical schoolteacher turned romantic,—he saw in it a means of salvation for the present world of his time. He longed too, for the return of a sage-king like Wen or Wu of the Chou dynasty, or like Yao, Shun, Yü, Tang,[2] all exemplary kings of antiquity noted for their great virtue, who ruled their subjects like loving parents, and who, by so doing, achieved a reign of peace and prosperity.

Not being a conjuror, Master K'ung could not bring to life the spirits of these great rulers of antiquity, but he could at least recreate with his imagination an idealized prince with all the perfect attributes of the former kings; and when that was done, he fell in love with his own creation. Would that such a sovereign might appear to make benevolent government once more a reality in the world! he must have fondly hoped. Perhaps, as we have previously hinted, he was hoping, too, that he himself might play the part of a worthy minister to such a sage-king! Needless to say, Master K'ung failed to find his ideal, but it is a testimony to his greatness that the ideal itself lives to this day.

4. *The Grass Bends with the Wind*

Master K'ung's greatest contribution to political philosophy lies in his effort to bring about harmonious relations between the ruler and the ruled. While considering class distinctions inalterable, he nevertheless worked for a closer and better understanding between the two. His only fault was that he failed to recognize in his scheme of government the worth and importance of the common people. To him, the masses did not matter; what mattered was the conduct of the ruler. This idea he expressed succinctly in the following words: "The prince (*chün-tzu*) is the wind, the common people (*hsiao-jen*) the grass, and the grass bends in the direction of the wind."

2. Yao and Shun were both legendary kings highly extolled for their virtue by the scholars of the K'ung school. Yü and Tang, also model sovereigns, were respectively founders of the two earliest Chinese dynasties Hsia and Shang.

The people, therefore, should be kept in their lowly place in a state of blissful ignorance. They should not be given any part in the government; they need not be told the reasons for the things they are ordered to do. The best they could expect was a wise and benevolent prince, who ruled with paternal authority as well as paternal kindness. Indeed, if the ruler were wise enough, he would not only govern his people with mere regulations and penalties, but he would also have their welfare at heart. This, moreover, could be easily achieved. What a ruler need do was to give his subjects enough to eat, for if the people had plenty, their prince would not be left alone in want; to spare them from heavy taxation; and to lead them into war after they had been instructed in its practice. From this we can also see that Master K'ung was no pacifist, however much he hated war.

The most important task of a sovereign, in the Master's opinion, was to gain the people's affection. In a famous passage that sounds surprisingly modern, the Master observed that the three essentials of good government were sufficient food, sufficient arms, and the confidence of the people.

"But," asked Tzu-kung, who had first raised the question, "if you had to part with one of the three, which would you give up?"

"Arms," answered the Master.

"But suppose," pursued Tzu-kung, "you are forced to forego one of the remaining two, which would you give up?"

"Food," replied the Master firmly. Then he continued, "From time immemorial, death has been the lot of us all, but a people that no longer trusts its ruler is lost indeed."

The essentials of government having been made clear, there still remains the question of how the ruler is to obtain the people's confidence. Master K'ung's answer is again simple and easy to execute. It is that the prince, as the head of his state, should so inspire the people by his noble conduct, that they

would "come to him of their own accord." "He who rules,"
asserted Master K'ung, "is like a pole-star, which abides in its
place, while all the other stars revolve respectfully around it."

Here again, in the hands of Master K'ung, the political
problem became one with the problem of moral cultivation on
the part of the ruler. For the higher the prince's authority, the
weightier his duty would be, and the greater, his virtue. He
was in such a pivotal position that just one move on his part
could sway his state either to prosperity or ruin. For instance,
if a sovereign refused to listen to good counsel, but insisted, in
spite of it, on putting his own ideas into practice, his stub-
bornness would ultimately cost him his kingdom.

As taught by Master K'ung, the nine basic duties of a prince
are as follows:

1. to cultivate himself
2. to honor men of worth
3. to be affectionate to his kinsmen
4. to respect great ministers
5. to treat with consideration all officials
6. to take fatherly care of the common people
7. to promote the hundred crafts
8. to be hospitable to strangers
9. to be friendly to the neighboring princes.[3]

In order to perform these offices, it became all the more im-
perative for a ruler to cultivate his personality,—the first and
the greatest of his duties,—for it was only when he himself was
morally perfect that he could win the people. To illustrate this
point, Master K'ung said: "Possessing virtue, a ruler possesses
men. Possessing men, he possesses the soil; possessing soil, he

3. This passage about the prince's duties is taken from the *Doctrine of the
Mean*, XX, 12. (Legge, *Chinese Classics*, I, 272–3.) Though the book, commonly
attributed to Tzu-ssu, Master K'ung's grandson, belongs to a later date, (See
Hughes, *The Great Learning & The Mean-in-Action*, pp. 86–100.) the passage
is in harmony with the teachings of the Master.

possesses wealth; possessing wealth, he possesses the means of government."

The moral attributes of a prince were the same as those of a gentleman, who, we remember, was originally a feudal lord himself. For a ruler, the cardinal virtues were also *li* (propriety), *yi* (righteousness), and *hsin* (good faith). "When a ruler loves *li*," said Master K'ung, "among the common people none will dare to be disrespectful. When a ruler loves *yi*, none will dare to be disobedient. When a ruler loves *hsin*, none will dare to conceal his true feelings. And when a ruler has all these virtues, people from the four quarters of the world will flock to him with their babies strapped on their backs."

But above all, a ruler should cultivate the supreme virtue of *jen* or "human-heartedness." *Jen* was the key-virtue with which a prince unlocked the people's hearts and possessed their loyalty. "There never has been a case," to quote a passage by a later disciple, "of a sovereign's possessing 'human-heartedness,' that those beneath him did not love righteousness. There never has been a case of the people's loving righteousness, that state affairs were not accomplished. And there never has been a case of the country's being well governed, that the wealth stored in coffers and treasuries did not continue in the sovereign's possession."[4] Thus we see that, whereas Master K'ung's emphasis had been mainly moral, his followers placed the emphasis on political economy. This is seen further in the assertion that for a reigning lord, "moral excellence is the root, and wealth the branch." The branches, of course, flourish only when the root is being cultivated for the flowering of the ruler's personality.

5. Ugh! Those Rice-Bags!

Between the ruler and his subjects was a great body of officials, who dealt directly with the people. They were the

4. *The Great Learning*, X, 21. (Legge, *The Chinese Classics*, I, 243.)

bridge, whereby the prince's orders were conveyed to his subjects. Important as it was for the prince to be benevolent, it was even more important that the officials be honest and capable. They were, in fact, the salesmen who sold to the people the ruler's goodness and kindness.

Since the preparation of young men for public service was his main task as a teacher, Master K'ung spoke with authority on the qualifications of a worthy official. His conversations with his students disclose a wealth of material on this subject. Though most of the ideas are obsolete, a few are still inspiring for a civil servant of the twentieth century. These may be summed up as moral integrity, loyalty to work, and unswerving attention to duty. "Once a gentleman has contrived to rectify his own conduct, he will have no difficulty in filling any government post. Whereas, if he cannot set an example himself, how can he expect to put others right?"

To be more specific, Master K'ung believed that a good minister should "utilize the services of his subordinates, overlook their minor faults, and promote those who are worthy and capable." As to his relations with the common people, an official should teach them by his example and never weary of doing his duty. Lastly, the Master had this advice for the aspiring young man: "Never be in a hurry; shut your eyes to small gains. Things done quickly cannot be done thoroughly, and seeking small advantages prevents one's accomplishing great things."

We must admit here that actually, there was a great disparity between Master K'ung's ideal minister and those who were on the government saddle. From his wide political experience, Master K'ung knew but too well the kind of corruption that had been going on in official circles. Recognizing that ignorance was at the root of much of this, he threw open the gates of learning to all young aspirants who desired to be instructed in the principles of government. And it is to Master

K'ung's credit that he did succeed in producing several model governors and loyal stewards.

In an interesting conversation with Tzu-kung, Master K'ung gave a good sketch of a model official and his unworthy counterpart.

"What must an official do to merit his name?" asked the disciple.

"He who shows a sense of honor in his private conduct, and he who does not disgrace his prince's commission when abroad, may be called a true official," replied the Master.

"May I ask who would rank next?"

"He who is praised for his filial piety by his kinsmen, and for his deference to elders by his fellow villagers."

"May I ask who would come next?"

"He who keeps his word and sticks to his course. A priggish little fellow, to be sure, yet perhaps he might come next."

"What would you say of present-day government officials?"

"Ugh!" exclaimed the Master. "Those rice-bags![5] They don't count at all."

6. *The Great Commonwealth*

Our discussion of Master K'ung's political philosophy would be incomplete without a word on his conception of the Great Society. From what we know of his political views, it is not difficult to see what his ideal state would be like.

As might be expected, in Master K'ung's Commonwealth, morality was the prevailing influence between the ruler and the ruled. On the one hand, the ruler should be morally good, so that he could diffuse his goodness among his people. The masses, on their part, should remain content in their passive role as subjects, in their humble employment, in their sufficiency, in their exemption from taxes and forced labor,—all

5. An equivalent in the colloquial Chinese language of the term *fan-t'ung,* people who know only how to fill their stomachs with rice.

in all, in the security of their lives and occupations. Hence, according to Master K'ung, the ideal world was a well-governed world, in which the people were well-behaved, the family well-regulated, and the society well-ordered,—a world, in which there would be the least suffering for humanity, with ample provisions for the poor, the sick, the aged, and the disabled,—a world, in which there would be a minimum of wars and other human tragedies. In other words, it was a world where peace and order thrived.

Indeed, this Great Society was not far to seek. It was right there in the pages of history, which told of the golden ages of antiquity, when sage-kings like Yao, Shun, Yü, Tang reigned. If these times seemed remote and their stories hard to prove, there was at least the splendid Chou dynasty itself, in the early days of which Kings Wen and Wu had ruled benevolently with the assistance of the great Duke. Master K'ung believed, and rightly so, that there must have been such a great reign in the past, which approached his ideals of perfect government. Thus it was natural for him,—what human being does not feel nostalgic for the good old days?—to long for those glorious periods recorded in history. And what could be more logical than to advocate reforms based on the idealized virtues of the past? Indeed, if the past was so perfect, why could it not be used as a pattern for the present and the future?

But what Master K'ung did not know was that neither did history repeat itself, nor could the past be recalled and imitated. What he failed to see was that he was living in a transitional period, in which old values and institutions were doomed to give place to the new,—an evolutionary process, which could not be stopped by any person, not even by the great Master himself. Since these changes were inevitable with the coming of every new era, so the present could never be the same as the past, and Master K'ung's dream remained forever a dream.

Nevertheless, his is a beautiful vision; and as visions go, a more tangible one than all the Republics, Utopias, and Atlantises put together. Indeed, we believe with Master K'ung that the glories of the past, however distant, had their basis in fact, and as such, will always remain in man's mind as long as man is dissatisfied with the present. The Utopia-makers, on the other hand, are mere visionaries, who create their brainchildren out of wistful thinking rather than the verisimilar facts of history. In comparison, therefore, the golden age of antiquity is more inspiring, calling forth men's best efforts to emulate it, because at least it did exist; while the Utopias and Republics are now just as disappointingly remote as when they were first pronounced some hundreds and thousands of years ago.

Master K'ung himself did not give us a picture of his ideal state. It was formulated for us a generation later in a superb passage attributed to him: "When the great *tao* flourished, the world was a common state, rulers were elected according to their wisdom and ability, and mutual confidence and peace prevailed. Therefore, people not only regarded their parents as parents, their children as children, but also those of others as their own. Old people were able to enjoy their old age; young men were able to employ their talents; juniors respected their elders; helpless widows, orphans, and cripples were well cared for. Men had their respective occupations, and women their homes . . . This was the period of the Great Commonwealth."

CHAPTER TWELVE

The Teacher of a Myriad
Generations—An Epilogue

1. *Great Is Master K'ung!*

IN ACCORDANCE WITH THE SAYING THAT "A MAN'S CASE CAN BE best judged after he is laid in the coffin," we shall now, after having presented the life and teachings of this most remarkable personality of all ages, make a final estimate of his place in history and his contributions to mankind. At first sight, this might seem a simple matter since we have such a vast literature on the subject to guide us in our task. But actually, the contrary is the case, for much of this critical material is confusing and misleading. As a matter of fact, the man K'ung Ch'iu has been so completely shrouded in the mist of time that only a dim and inaccurate outline of his life is perceptible. His teaching, too, has been greatly distorted, while the philosophy that now bears his name is a heterogeneous admixture of many elements. Master K'ung, perhaps more than anybody else, has suffered misrepresentation at the hands of friend and foe alike. From this unhappy lot, to be sure, no great man can escape, but Master K'ung was especially a victim of this vice.

It may seem paradoxical to observe in this connection that it was Master K'ung's devoted followers who sinned most against him. The fact is that these votaries, obsessed by the idea of their Master's holiness, have erected a golden statue of their idol, crowned him like a king, and enveloped him with the halos of a godhead. A magnificent tribute, no doubt; but unfortunately, the real K'ung Ch'iu was neither king nor divinity, but a plain member of the *shih* (official-scholar) class, intelligent, well-educated, and above all else, supremely human. A matter of lasting regret it is that, because of this process of gilding, the true character of Master K'ung was obscured, and now after 25 centuries it is almost impossible to restore with accuracy or vividness the historical K'ung Ch'iu.

Bearing this in mind, we have endeavored in our account of the Master's life to sift the facts from myth. In so doing, we have tried to be as critical as possible. While it is obvious that all this enthronement and deification of the real K'ung Ch'iu is sheer nonsense, we are also aware, on the other hand, of the absurdity of stripping the Master of all his trappings and making him a lean scarecrow. By thus taking the middle course, the golden mean, of which Master K'ung was so high in his praise, we have presented from our own observation what we believe to be a genuine picture of the Master, independent of any earlier criticism. It is gratifying to find that the Sage as we have depicted him, with all his aspirations and accomplishments as well as his foibles and failures, is at least human, and therefore great!

2. *His Merits Assessed*

If we are to estimate the merits of an historical personage, the one sure criterion is that of his worth in relation to his own age as well as to all time. In our appraisal of Master K'ung, we should, therefore, ask ourselves two questions: How well did he appear in the eyes of his own generation? And how well does he stand the test of time? These are pertinent questions, in the answers to which will be revealed the true worth of the man.

While taking stock of Master K'ung's merits, let us confine

ourselves to his moral and political teachings, in which he was truly outstanding. In the previous chapters, we have dwelt at large on Master K'ung's contributions in these fields. We now propose to study the subject from a single point of view. We are here concerned with the Master's doctrine as a whole, and we want to find out wherein its greatness lies.

First of all, we must reiterate our belief that Master K'ung was essentially a product of the feudal age, and should be judged as such. Rather than leading the way for the future, he advocated a return to antiquity, of which he was the best representative. But here something short of a miracle happened. Master K'ung, we know, was a traditionalist. It is hard to say whether it is the conservative nature of the Chinese people that has found Master K'ung's teachings so congenial, or it is the Master's great influence that has swayed the Chinese to this side of conservatism. In either case, it is astonishing to note that Master K'ung, epitome of the past, should have remained so long, notwithstanding all the great changes that have taken place in the country, a pattern for Chinese life and thought. The philosophy of the K'ung school, to be sure, has been modified from time to time by the introduction of new elements, but Master K'ung, its originator, has continued to be the one great living force throughout the centuries.

The secret of Master K'ung's success, as already pointed out, lies in his broad humanity, in his practical wisdom, and in the universality of his teaching. These sparkling virtues cast into the shadows whatever personal limitations he had. Sometimes he was even able to turn his feudal idiosyncrasies to advantage, as when he changed *li* from an out-worn code of aristocracy to a fresh set of rules for polite society. As such, *li* remains a vital influence to this day, as is shown in the genteel manners of the Chinese people. In the same way, Master K'ung's insistence on paternal government, though no longer tenable because of the growing size of the country, served at least as a guiding principle to the rulers of later dynasties. And, of course, Master K'ung's great triumph came when he changed *chün-tzu*, a Chou aristocrat, to a gentleman endowed with all human virtues.

Most important of all, there is also that grand conception of *jen*, the consummation of the man-to-man relationship, that Master K'ung contributed to ethics. It is grand, but not grandiose like the teaching of all-embracing love advocated by Mo Ti,[1] a later rival of Master K'ung. Whereas universal love might be a loftier ideal, *jen* is more practical and within the reach of everyone. So it is exactly here that Master K'ung excels all the other teachers of men, Christ and Buddha not excepted. The real K'ung Ch'iu, though without the benefit of divinity, is nevertheless dearer to us, because he is one of us; he speaks our language and thinks our thoughts. Essentially human himself, Master K'ung is just as much concerned with worldly problems as we are; and possessing the same shortcomings that we have, he too is groping his way towards perfection. That is why his teachings speak directly to our hearts and find there a warm response. The wisest of all men in his own age, the Master still beckons to us with his mature wisdom that sparkles in spite of the gathering dust of time.

3. *His Influence Surveyed*

Master K'ung's greatness can also be measured by the extent, intensity, and duration of his influence. Suffering only a brief eclipse in the Ch'in dynasty (221–206 B.C.), whose First Emperor was notorious for his burning of books and the burying alive of scholars, Master K'ung became in the later centuries the greatest influence in China. His doctrine was accepted as state dogma; his works, namely the books of *Changes,*

1. Mo Ti (B.C. 480?–390?) was founder of the famous Chinese philosophy of universal love called Mohism. (See Y. P. Mei, *The Ethical and Political Works of Motse,* London, 1929; and his *Motse, the Neglected Rival of Confucius,* London, 1934.)

Poetry, History, and *Rites,* all of which he edited, and the *Spring and Autumn,* which he compiled, were elevated as Classics to be studied by students in both private and public schools. In fact, these were also the subjects studied for the civil service examination that led eventually to the broad avenues of officialdom.

The monopoly of learning by the K'ung scholars has been unparalleled in history. To be sure, in the decades immediately following Master K'ung there did emerge a number of philosophic schools like Taoism, Mohism, Dialecticism, and Legalism, etc. to compete with the orthodox teachings of Master K'ung. But in the course of time, these were completely overshadowed, and soon disappeared altogether from the scene. Only Taoism, founded by Lao Tzu, afforded any sort of effectual competition. But it too degenerated from a philosophical system to mere superstition; and though its religious elements gained a large following among the credulous, and its metaphysical ideas attracted the skeptic in times of disorder, Taoism as a way of thought never offered any serious threat to the supremacy of the K'ung dogma. Buddhism, which entered China from India in a much later period and had its heyday in the 4th and 5th centuries, proved to be a powerful rival of Taoism in matters celestial and speculative, but it could never match the K'ung doctrine as a form of ethical and political philosophy. Thus, the dominant position held by Master K'ung in China's intellectual life has continued unchallenged for almost twenty-five centuries until the present day. •

The effect of this K'ung dictatorship in Chinese thought has been far-reaching. For one thing, it has left indelible marks on the social and political structure of the nation. With the educational system firmly under their control, the K'ung teachers succeeded in inculcating the doctrines of their school on the minds of the young people. As these grew up, they were awarded, after a successful competition in the Classics, key positions in the government as court officials and provincial administrators. Then came their turn to recruit new members to be similarly indoctrinated. Thus the process went on until the entire Chinese bureaucracy was filled with K'ung scholars. From their solidly entrenched positions they were never budged except in times of foreign conquest or usurpation of imperial powers by the eunuchs, who were, as history reveals, inveterate enemies of the literati. These, however, were rare occasions, and as a whole, the Chinese government has been actually run by the scholar-officials of the K'ung school for the last twenty centuries or more ever since the Han dynasty (206 B.C.–A.D. 220), when the doctrine of the Master was first made orthodox.

Moreover, the K'ung philosophy has molded the character of the Chinese people. Their mentality as well as their outlook on life has been immensely colored by the Master's ideas, which have been formulated since his day into a governing code of etiquette and morality for all the Chinese. Dynasties have risen and fallen, but the K'ung ethical system, however stereotyped it might become, abided, in spite of these changes, the one enduring influence in Chinese life. Likewise, because of the sanctions received from Master K'ung, the large family system, with a special stress on filial and fraternal obedience on the part of its younger members, continued to be a dominant factor in society. All in all, in almost everything from their national to private life, in their culture, in their manners and behavior, in their customs and traditions, in their mode of expression in speaking and writing, the Chinese have been greatly indebted to Master K'ung. It is no exaggeration then to say that it is the Master's teachings that have welded together the Chinese nation.

4. His Position Affirmed: "The Greatest Teacher of Antiquity"

All that we have said above is true up to the first years of the twentieth century. But now as we approach its second half on this significant occasion of the 2500th anniversary of Master K'ung's birth, things have changed so rapidly in China that with the advent of a new era, we have also to readjust our attitude towards this great historical figure. Today, everything old is being revaluated in the light of modern knowledge. How would it fare with Master K'ung, a feudal apologist and patron saint of the emperors, after a most careful examination of his credentials by the new Republic?

A wide difference of opinions results. They range from those of the Master's devoted partisans, who wanted to establish the K'ung dogma as a state religion and the Master as its titulary head, to the others, who diametrically opposed to the first, consider Master K'ung as the source of all the trouble in a disorderly and weakened country. "Down with Master K'ung and his Company," is the slogan of the latter group. Between these two extremes is found the general attitude, which, while accepting Master K'ung as a sage and considering some of his teachings as still valid, nevertheless refuses to believe that Master K'ung could be the savior of the modern world. So far, in regard to the exact position the Master holds in contemporary China, critical opinion today has not yet crystallized. Hence the present work was undertaken in an attempt to give the Master his rightful place in history only, while making a clean sweep of present and future speculation.

From our point of view, Master K'ung was primarily a teacher of antiquity. He wins our admiration not merely because of the content of his teachings, but also because of his pedagogical methods, his attitude towards students, and especially, because of his unswerving devotion to the great and honorable profession of teaching. It was Master K'ung who, as the reader may remember, first rescued ancient culture from its degeneration in the hands of court officials, and gave it a new lease of life. It was Master K'ung who brought learning, hitherto confined to the prince's court and aristocratic household, to a wider public. It was also Master K'ung who paved the way for equality in education by giving to all who had the desire and capacity for knowledge, irrespective of their rank and means, an opportunity to be educated. In his insistence on "education without class" and in his acceptance of poor but qualified students,—we readily recall that most of his good students came from poor families,—Master K'ung was truly the greatest of all teachers.

As an advocate of morality, Master K'ung's one great mission in life was to work for the improvement of the people. It was only in his effort to combat the moral decay of his times that he got interested in politics and took it up as a means to an end; it was also for the same reason that, when neglected by the prince of his own state, he travelled abroad to seek employment with other rulers. But in both his term of office and in his wanderings, he never neglected to cultivate himself and to teach, for teaching was his life-long profession.

Obviously, Master K'ung's political ideas had never been sound and progressive, based as they were upon feudal tradition. Furthermore, in the course of time, they suffered much pandering in the hands of politicians and emperors, who used the Master's great authority to justify their autocratic rule and to gain the support of the scholar-officials. On the other hand, the Master's ethical teachings were far more attractive. In them we can still find an inexhaustible store of wisdom as well as a useful set of rules for good living. But even these are outmoded today because of the upheavals in Chinese life as a result of the dynamic impact of the West. With the entire fabric of Chinese society shaken to the ground and the shape of things to come so uncertain, it is yet premature to predict what chances there are of the Master's retaining his hold on the moral life of the Chinese people.

Of one thing, however, we are certain. Should the great honor and high respect formerly shown to Master K'ung continue in the future, it would be not for his merits as a statesman or moralist, but for his role as an inspiring and indefatigable teacher. Foremost among the mentors of men, he was also assuredly the most successful,—witness the vast number of his immediate disciples and the millions of his later followers, all of them attracted to him not by the promise of reward in a future life, but the genuine goodness of his words in relation to this life. Yes, as a teacher Master K'ung reigns supreme: his achievement is great, his position secure, his enthusiasm unmatched, and his noble work of preserving ancient literature worthy of the highest praise,—in all these the Master affords an illustrious example to the people of all generations.

A Selected Bibliography

I. CHINESE HISTORY, PHILOSOPHY, AND RELIGION

A. HISTORY AND CULTURE

Fitzgerald, C. P., *China, a Short Cultural History* (rev. ed.), N. Y., 1950.

Goodrich, L. Carrington, *A Short History of the Chinese People* (rev. ed.), N. Y., 1951.

Granet, Marcel, *Chinese Civilization*, London, 1930.

Hirth, Friedrich, *The Ancient History of China to the End of the Chou Dynasty*, N. Y., 1908.

MacNair, Harley F. (Ed.), *China*, Berkeley, California, 1946.

Zen, Sophia H. Chen (Ed.), *Symposium on Chinese Culture*, Shanghai, 1931.

B. PHILOSOPHY AND THOUGHT

Carus, Paul, *Chinese Thought*, Chicago, 1907.

Chan, Wing-tsit, *An Outline and a Bibliography of Chinese Philosophy*, Hanover, New Hampshire, 1953.

Creel, H. G., *Chinese Thought from Confucius to Mao Tse-tung*, Chicago, 1953.

Creel, H. G., *Sinism: a Study of the Evolution of the Chinese World View*, Chicago, 1929.

Fung Yu-lan, *A History of Chinese Philosophy* (tran. by D. Bodde), 2 vols., Princeton, 1952–3.

Fung Yu-lan, *A Short History of Chinese Philosophy*, N. Y., 1948.

Fung Yu-lan, *The Spirit of Chinese Philosophy* (tran. by E. R. Hughes), London, 1947.

Hughes, E. R., *Chinese Philosophy in Classical Times*, London, 1942.

Liang Chi-chao, *History of Chinese Political Thought during the Early Tsin Period*, London, 1930.

Lin Mousheng, *Men and Ideas: An Informal History of Chinese Political Thought*, N. Y., 1942.

Suzuki, D. T., *A Brief History of Early Chinese Philosophy*, London, 1914.

Waley, Arthur, *Three Ways of Thought in Ancient China*, London, 1939.

Wang Gung-hsing, *The Chinese Mind*, N. Y., 1946.

Wei, Francis C. M., *The Spirit of Chinese Culture*, N. Y., 1947.

Wright, Arthur F. (Ed.), *Studies in Chinese Thought*, Chicago, 1953.

C. RELIGION

Chan, Wing-tsit, *Religious Trends in Modern China*, N. Y., 1953.

De Groot, J. J. M., *Religion in China*, N. Y., 1912.

Hughes, E. R. and Hughes, K., *Religion in China*, London, 1950.

Legge, James, *The Religions of China*, London, 1880.

Soothill, W. E., *The Three Religions of China*, London, 1929.

Weber, Max, *The Religions of China; Confucianism and Taoism* (tran. by H. H. Gerth), Glencoe, Illinois, 1951.

Yang, Y. C., *China's Religious Heritage*, N. Y., 1943.

II. CONFUCIUS AND CONFUCIANISM

Alexander, G. G., *Confucius, the Great Teacher*, London, 1890.

Brown, Brian, *The Story of Confucius, His Life and Sayings*, Philadelphia, 1927.

Chen Huan-chang. *The Economic Principles of Confucius and His School*, 2 vols., N. Y., 1911.

Cheng Tien-hsi, *China Moulded by Confucius*, London, 1946.

Collis, Maurice, *The First Holy One*, N. Y., 1948.

Creel, H. G., *Confucius, the Man and the Myth*, N. Y., 1949.

Crow, Carl, *Master K'ung, the Story of Confucius*, N. Y. 1938.

Dawson, Miles, *Ethics of Confucius*, N. Y., 1915.

Dubs, Homer H., "The Dates of Confucius' Birth," *Asia Major,* N.S. I, Pt. II, London, 1949.

Faber, Ernest, *A Systematic Digest of the Doctrines of Confucius* (tran. by P. G. von Mollendorff), Shanghai?, 1902?

Giles, Herbert A., *Confucianism and Its Rivals,* London, 1915.

Hsu, Leonard Shihlien, *The Political Philosophy of Confucianism,* London, 1932.

Koehn, Alfred, *Confucius: His Life and Work,* Peking, 1945.

Liu Wu-chi, *A Short History of Confucian Philosophy,* Harmondsworth, England, 1955.

Shryock, John K., *The Origin and Development of the State Cult of Confucius,* N. Y., 1932.

Starr, Frederick, *Confucianism,* N. Y., 1930.

Watters, T., *A Guide to the Tablets in a Temple of Confucius,* Shanghai, 1879.

Wilhelm, Richard, *Confucius and Confucianism,* (tran. by George E. Danton and Annina P. Danton), N. Y., 1931.

Yetts, W. Percival, *The Legend of Confucius,* London, 1943.

Wu, John C. H., "The Real Confucius," *Tien Hsia,* vol. I, Shanghai, 1935.

III. CONFUCIAN CLASSICS

Chen, Ivan, *The Book of Filial Piety,* London, 1908.

Hughes, E. R., *The Great Learning & The Mean-in-Action,* London, 1942.

Kramers, Robert Paul, *K'ung Tzu Chia Yü; The School Sayings of Confucius,* Leiden, 1949.

Legge, James, *The Chinese Classics,* 5 vols. in 8, Hongkong, 1861–72.
    Vol. 1. "The Prolegomena"; *Confucian Analects; The Great Learning; The Doctrine of the Mean*
    Vol. 2. *The Works of Mencius*
    Vol. 3. *The Shoo King; or, The Book of Historical Documents*
    Vol. 4. *The She King; or, The Book of Poetry*
    Vol. 5. *The Chun Tsew (Spring and Autumn),* with *The Tso Chuen (Tso's Commentary)*

Legge, James, *The Sacred Books of China: The Texts of Confucianism* (in *The Sacred Books of the East,* ed. by F. Max Muller), Oxford, 1879–85.

    Vol. 3. *The Shu King (The Book of Historical Documents)*

          The Religious Portion of *The Shih King (The Book of Poetry)*

          The Hsiao King (The Book of Filial Piety)

    Vol. 16. *The Yih King (The Book of Changes)*

    Vol. 27. *The Li Ki (The Book of Rites)*

Lin Yutang, *The Wisdom of Confucius,* N. Y., 1938.

Lyall, Leonard, *The Sayings of Confucius,* London, 1909.

Soothill, William E., *The Analects of Confucius,* London, 1937.

Steele, John, *The I-Li; or, Book of Etiquette and Ceremonial,* 2 vols., London, 1917.

Waddell, Helen, *Lyrics from the Chinese,* N. Y., 1935.

Waley, Arthur, *The Analects of Confucius,* N. Y., 1939.

Waley, Arthur, *The Book of Songs,* London, 1937.

Wilhelm, Richard, *The I Ching or the Book of Changes,* New York, 1950

Index

185